SpringerBriefs in Computer Science

Series Editors
Stan Zdonik
Peng Ning
Shashi Shekhar
Jonathan Katz
Xindong Wu
Lakhmi C. Jain
David Padua
Xuemin Shen
Borko Furht

For further volumes:
http://www.springer.com/series/10028

Simone Campanoni

Guide to ILDJIT

 Springer

Dr. Simone Campanoni
Department of Engineering and Applied Sciences
Harvard University
Oxford Street 33
Cambridge
MA 02138
USA
e-mail: xan@eecs.harvard.edu

ISSN 2191-5768   e-ISSN 2191-5776
ISBN 978-1-4471-2193-0   e-ISBN 978-1-4471-2194-7
DOI 10.1007/978-1-4471-2194-7
Springer London Dordrecht Heidelberg New York

British Library Cataloguing in Publication Data
A catalogue record for this book is available from the British Library

Library of Congress Control Number: 2011936140

Cover design: eStudio Calamar, Berlin/Figueres

Printed on acid-free paper

Springer is part of Springer Science+Business Media (www.springer.com)

Il bruco, mediante l'esercitato studio di tessere con mirabile artificio e sottile lavoro intorno a sè la nova abitazione, esce poi fori di quella colle dipinte e belle ali, con quelle lanciandosi verso il cielo

Leonardo da Vinci

Foreword

We are all familiar with the time-honored idea of a Virtual Machine that is neutral with respect to computer architecture and can be used to execute a high-level language, after its translation to the VM byte-code. This approach can be found in several successful mono-language systems, that support popular languages such as Java or SmallTalk. Such systems combine interpretation with dynamic translation, including code optimization, to achieve higher performance.

Other more ambitious VMs support many languages, and the best known example of a source-language neutral VM is the Common Language Infrastructure (standard ECMA 335 or ISO/IEC 23271), available from the .NET proprietary system and from free open-source projects including the most established Mono and, more recently, ILDJIT. Let me disclaim any responsibility for this unpronounceable acronym that I had urged Simone to change, before the fast growing popularity of the system made renaming inconvenient—would you imagine repainting a boat name while she sails on a successful regatta? Yet the D for distributed reveals that this VM belongs to a new generation that from the very start was designed for parallel execution.

Since the early developments at the Formal Languages and Compiler Group, Simone shaped the software structure to be modular and extensible, so that other team members, including graduate students, could easily contribute new plug-ins. Two distinguishing objectives of the early ILDJIT were the emphasis on embedded applications running on small microprocessors, motivated by the support of chip manufacturer STMicroelectronics, and the use of C both as application and compiler implementation language.

The long way of the project status from curiosity to recognition and to adoption by other research labs and developers has been punctuated by visible progresses in terms of language and test suites coverage, reduction of residual errors, and, more than anything else, by performance improvements that rank ILDJIT at the top of CLI-based systems in many relevant cases.

In the last two years the project direction has moved to Harvard University where new and exciting developments have happened, the most original ones not yet documented in this book because under scientific investigation; I mention friendlier user interfaces, a range of inter-procedural optimizations, the option to use the compiler ahead-of-time (i.e. statically), compatibility with byte-codes generated by Microsoft .NET front-end compilers, and porting of the system on MS Windows operating system. All that makes ILDJIT an attractive choice for a compilation platform, whenever, in addition to language and machine independence, run-time adaptation and program transformations are important. Future users and developers will find this timely handbook a practical companion. Please Simone, now take some rest before you commit yourself to some ambitious new development!

Politecnico di Milano, June 2011   Stefano Crespi Reghizzi

Acknowledgments

This book is the product of six years of both engineering works and researches during which I had the privilege to share these efforts with the enlightened Prof. Stefano Crespi Reghizzi, for whom I will be always thankful.

After the Ph.D. at Politecnico di Milano, I moved to Harvard University to work with both Prof. David Brooks and Prof. Gu-Yeon Wei; we have worked to improve ILDJIT to be useful for the extremely exciting researches we are doing together. I would like to thank Prof. David Brooks and Prof. Gu-Yeon Wei both to have given me the opportunity of working with them and for advising me in such a great and remarkable way.

Any work of such breadth necessarily builds on efforts of more than one author; at the head of this list of people, which gave me a priceless help, there are Andrea Di Biagio, Martino Sykora, Michele Tartara, Ettore Speziale, Stefano Anelli and Luca Rocchini.

I would like to thank Andrea Cazzaniga, which was the first reader of this book.

Last, but not least, I would like to thank all my family, especially my mom Bruna and my brother Luca, who both always believe in me, no matter what, and helped me to continue my university studies at Politecnico di Milano.

Contents

Chapter 1
Introduction

Abstract After an introduction of the compilation framework named ILDJIT, the history of this project is outlined. The major features of ILDJIT are highlighted for an easy comparison with other compilation frameworks.

Keywords Compilation framework · ILDJIT · Dynamic compilation · Static compilation · Bytecode system

This book is a guide to getting started with Intermediate Language Distributed Just In Time (ILDJIT), a compilation framework designed to be both easily extensible and easily configurable.

This framework can be used to build our own tool chains by customizing ILDJIT for our specific purposes. Customizations can be used for both static and dynamic compilers already included inside the framework. These extensions can be implemented once to be later used inside every compiler available inside the framework. Moreover, customizations allow us to modify both the behaviors and the characteristics of these compilers to best satisfy our specific needs.

Currently, ILDJIT is able to translate bytecode programs to generate machine code for both Intel x86 and ARM processors for both Windows and Linux operating systems. By relying on ILDJIT technology, more input languages, or platforms, can be supported.

After providing a brief history of ILDJIT, its major features are introduced. Next chapters describe ILDJIT in more details to understand how to use it. Moreover, this guide introduces and describes how this framework can be exploited by extending it to match specific requirements. Examples of extensions of the framework are provided by using the C language. Moreover, C and C# languages are used in this book to write programs, which are compiled through ILDJIT eventually. This book does not attempt to teach either C or C# languages themselves, since this material can be found in many other places. Finally, design choices followed towards ILDJIT during our multi-years development efforts are introduced and discussed.

S. Campanoni, *Guide to ILDJIT*, SpringerBriefs in Computer Science,
DOI: 10.1007/978-1-4471-2194-7_1, © Simone Campanoni 2011

1.1 A Brief History of ILDJIT

The original author of the ILDJIT compiler is Simone Campanoni.

The project started in late October 2005 when Simone introduced his wish to develop a dynamic compiler for the bytecode CIL to Prof. Stefano Crespi Reghizzi, who, with a endless enthusiasm, advised Simone through both his master thesis and his Ph.D., at Politecnico di Milano. During this period, Simone, with the priceless help of several students of Prof. Crespi Reghizzi, built the compiler leading to its first releases. In particular, the first one was made in August 2007. This release was the first step to prove the potentiality of the project, and in particular, it provided a compiler ables to exploit the parallelism available inside multiprocessor platforms. During this period, the project was supported by chip manufacturer STMicroelectronics.

After the Ph.D., Simone with both Prof. David Brooks and Prof. Gu-Yeon Wei continued the development of ILDJIT at Harvard University improving it to a mature framework ables to compile bytecode programs in several different compilation schemes by optimizing the produced code aggressively. A major revision of the compilation framework came with the 0.4 series in 2010, which added the ability to translate code inside both dynamic and static compilation schemes.

Over time ILDJIT has been extended becoming a compilation framework, which includes more and more compilation schemes including the classic ones. Its development is still guided by Simone Campanoni, which relies on it for his own researches at Harvard University.

1.2 Major Features of ILDJIT

The use of a virtual machine language, instead of machine code, is by now a well-established and successful technique for porting programs across different hardware platforms, without incurring into the difficulties and draw-backs of software distribution, when done at source-language level. In addition, interoperability between different source languages is made possible by their translation into a common suitable virtual code. Java bytecode first, and then *CLI (Common Language Infrastructure)* are the *de facto* industrial standards for such virtualization of the Instruction Set Architecture. In particular CLI, after its international standardization as ECMA 335 [1] and ISO/IEC 23271:2006, has become a very attractive framework, where applications written in multiple high-level languages, including also unmanaged language like C, can be executed in different system environments, at no cost for adaptation.

The increasing acceptance of CLI, also in areas traditionally reserved to direct compilation into machine code, is witnessed by the growth and consolidation over the years of the tool chains needed to support virtualization, namely static front-end compilers translating popular source languages into virtual code, and Virtual Execution Systems (VES), such as .NET, Mono, and Portable.Net. Although the first VES's were based on code interpretation, all modern ones use instead Dynamic Compilation, in order to achieve better performances.

A VES is a very complex software system that takes years for his development and in a sense is never finished, since new requirements keep coming from the advances in machine architectures, source languages, operating systems and middleware. Therefore it is not surprising that the current generation of VES has been designed having in mind the desktop personal computers and the traditional embedded systems, before the advent of multi-core architectures and single-chip multiprocessors, and without taking into consideration the great opportunities they offer for parallelization inside the VES and between VES and application.

The new free software VES that we present here is named ILDJIT [2] translator, which is especially intended for parallel architectures. Moreover, it is flexible enough to easily adapt to the evolving, and hard to anticipate, requirements of modern computer platforms. ILDJIT is designed to be easily extensible by providing a framework where existing modules can be substituted by user customized ones.

Our project from the very start in 2005 focused on multi-processors and aimed at offering a complete framework to study the different components of a dynamic compiler and their interactions in such environments. We believe our experience should be of interest to anyone considering porting or designing a virtual machine and dynamic compiler for a directly interpretable representation (such as CIL or Java bytecode) to a multi-processor architecture.

It is obvious that on a computer with more processors than application threads, the VES can run uninterrupted on a processor, so that many compilation/application balancing problems found on single processor machine simply disappear. In order to take full advantage of the high degree of parallelism of both current and future platforms, we designed the compiler framework as a parallel program. Compiler parallelism is manifold. First, the compiler phases are organized as a pipeline so that several CIL methods can be simultaneously compiled by different compilation phases.

Second, since many kinds of optimizations are applied in static compilers, and it is not a priori known which of them are more effective in either a dynamic setting or in different domains, we decided to design separate optimizers as processes running on a common Intermediate Representation.

Third, the VES software architecture ought to be flexible and open to an unpredictable number of new modules, as the project progresses and experience tells us which optimizations are productive for which applications. Moreover, flexibility is needed to choose the most performing solution from a set of alternative algorithms, depending on the application profile and needs: an example is garbage collection for dynamic memory allocation, where our system has four supports to automatically choose from. To obtain flexibility and modularity most modules are implemented as plugins. The entire system architecture is designed according to the software engineering principles of *design patterns* [3].

One could fear that a compiler implemented as a distributed and dynamically linkable program would have to pay a high overhead, to the point that the benefit from hardware parallelism might be offset especially for a small number of processors. On the contrary our experiments show that the performance of applications compiled by our system are comparable to some of the best known VES's, on a single processor machine, and superior on multi processor platforms. Of course we did benefit from part of the experience of earlier systems in such critical matters as granularity of compilation unit, unit compilation scheduling, optimization, memory management, and processor re-targeting.

1.3 Conventions Used in This Book

This guide contains several examples, which can be typed at the keyboard. A command entered at the terminal is shown like this,

```
$ command
```

In case a command produces an output, it is printed next to it, like in the following case:

```
$ echo "ILDJIT"
ILDJIT
```

The first character on the first line, the dollar sign $, is the terminal prompt, and should not be typed.

Both the code and source files used in this guide can be entered by hand using any text editor, such as vi or emacs. The example programs should work with any version of ILDJIT. Please refer to Appendix for any trouble.

The examples provided in this guide were tested on a GNU operating system running on top of an Intel x86 based platform. Some non-essential and verbose system-dependent output messages have been edited in the examples for brevity by inserting a sequence of dots "...".

References

1. ECMA ECMA-335: common language infrastructure (CLI). http://www.ecma-international. org/publications/files/ECMA-ST/Ecma-335.pdf (2010). Cited 11 June 2011
2. Campanoni, S., Agosta, G., Crespi-Reghizzi S., Biagio A.D.: A highly flexible, parallel virtual machine: design and experience of ILDJIT. In: Software: Practice and Experience, pp. 177–207 Wiley (2010)
3. Gamma, E., Helm, R., Johnson, R., Vlissides, J.: Design patterns: elements of reusable object-oriented software. Addison-Wesley, Reading (1995)

Chapter 2
Generating, Compiling and Executing Bytecode Programs

Abstract The generation of CIL programs—input of ILDJIT—is an important step of the compilation process described inside this book. This chapter describes how to generate CIL code by using available tools, such as Mono and GCC4CLI. Moreover, compilation processes available in ILDJIT are described including both static and dynamic compilations.

Keywords CIL programs · Compile bytecode programs · Compilation framework · Just-in-time compilation · Dynamic look-ahead compilation · Dynamic compilation · Static compilation · Bytecode systems

Compilers consider programs written by using a source language, such as C, C++, Java, and so on, to generate their semantically equivalent representations by targeting a destination language, such as the machine code of a target platform (e.g. Intel x86). In order to start using them, examples of programs written by using their source language have to be provided.

ILDJIT [1] is able both to translate programs written in CIL [2] bytecode language and execute them on Intel x86 and ARM platforms. Therefore, in order to use this framework, we need to produce the input of ILDJIT: CIL programs.

CIL is a stack-based bytecode language with a rich set of metadata, which includes descriptions of data types. Even if it is possible to write CIL programs by using a normal text editor, such as vi or emacs, and encode them to its binary format described in the ECMA-335 [2] standard, the author of this book suggests to the reader to use available tools to generate them automatically by starting from more human readable programming languages like C [3], C++ [4], Java [5] or C# [6] to avoid possible headaches.

This chapter starts by describing how to generate CIL programs from C or C# programs and it continues by introducing the compilation process of ILDJIT, which leads to the generation of the target machine code eventually. Different compilation schemes are available to the user of ILDJIT, which can decide the set of compilation

S. Campanoni, *Guide to ILDJIT*, SpringerBriefs in Computer Science,   5
DOI: 10.1007/978-1-4471-2194-7_2, © Simone Campanoni 2011

steps to perform offline (i.e., static compilation) and the ones to perform when the program is running (i.e., dynamic compilation).

2.1 Generating the Bytecode

In order to describe how to generate CIL programs, we start writing one of the simplest program from the user of a programming language point of view, which is also one of the first milestone for a compiler developer: the famous Hello world program. After the introduction of its implementation in two different languages, C and C#, we generate their correspondent CIL representations to highlight the impact of the source language to the CIL program.

By using an editor like vi, we write the following program and we save it to the file called hello_world.c:

```
/* hello_world.c */
#include <stdio.h>
int main () {
   printf("Hello, world!\n");
   return 0;
}
```

To produce the CIL bytecode from C programs, we rely on the GCC based compiler called GCC4CLI [7]. In particular, in order to compile our C program, we run the following command:

```
$ cil32-gcc -o hello_world_c.cil hello_world.c
```

The result is a file called hello_world_c.cil, which is the CIL representation of our hello world program. This file can be used as input to ILDJIT, which first produces and then executes the correspondent machine code. In order to run CIL programs, the ILDJIT command iljit is used and its syntax is the following:

```
iljit ILDJIT_OPTIONS FILE_CIL ARGUMENTS_OF_CIL_PROGRAM
```

In our case, the hello world program has no parameter and we do not use ILDJIT options for its execution. Hence,

```
$ iljit hello_world_c.cil
Hello, world!
```

Notice that we cannot execute CIL programs directly on our underlying platform because it does not know how to interpret them.

As next example, we generate the CIL representation of a hello world program by using the C# programming language. By using our editor, we write the following file called hello_world.cs:

```
/* hello_world.cs */
using System;
public class HelloWorld {
public static int Main () {
  Console.Write("Hello, world!\n");
  return 0;
  }
}
```

In order to produce the CIL representation of our C# program, we rely on the Mono [8] compiler.

```
$ mcs -out:hello_world_cs.cil hello_world.cs
```

The result is a file called hello_world_cs.cil, which is the CIL representation of our C# hello world program. As before, the generated file is given as input to ILDJIT.

```
$ iljit hello_world_cs.cil
Hello, world!
```

Since from two different programming languages, C and C#, we generate two different CIL programs that produce the same output, one question could arise: what are the differences between these two CIL programs? To answer this question, we compare those two programs: hello_world_c.cil and hello_world_cs.cil. A deeper analysis on these files (following described) shows that they differ quite substantially. This difference exists for two reasons: first these files are produced starting from different programming languages, C and C#. The second reason is due to the different compiler used to produce them: GCC4CLI and Mono. Our analysis is based on the output of the tool monodis [8] available inside the Mono project. Following we report the important fraction of its output when it is applied to hello_world_cs.cil.

```
$ monodis ./hello_world_cs.cil
...
.method public static int32 Main () cil managed {
  ldstr "Hello, world!\n"
  call void class System.Console::Write(string)
  ldc.i4.0
  ret
}
...
```

The CIL is composed by one method, Main, which is the entry point of the program (i.e., the first method executed). Inside this method, there is a call to another one, Write, which belongs to an external CIL library called Base Class Library

(BCL), which is defined inside the ECMA-335 standard. The method `Write` prints to the terminal the string given as its input eventually.

Let us consider the CIL hello world program coming from the C language: `hello_world_cs.cil`. As before, we use `monodis` to analyze the file. The important fraction of its output is the following:

```
$ monodis ./hello_world_c.cil
...
.method public static int32 main () cil managed {
  ldsflda valuetype string_type hello_world_c::string 0
  call int32 libstd::puts(int8*)
  pop
  ldc.i4 0
  ret
}
...
```

We can notice two important differences comparing it to the previous case: the function called to print the string is different. Instead of calling `Write`, the method `main` calls `puts`, which belongs to an external CIL library produced by the GCC4CLI compiler, that maps calls to the standard C library to the ones available in BCL. We can assign this mismatch to the differences between the two programming languages used. The second difference is related to the string to print. This time, the mismatch is due to the fact that different compilers have been used to generate the CIL.

2.2 Static Compilation

ILDJIT provides a compilation scheme that exposes the benefits of the static compilation by exploiting the more and more predominant multicore technology. After describing what a static compilation scheme is, we introduce and motivate its specific implementation available inside ILDJIT.

Usually, static compilation refers to the compilation process where the correspondent machine code of a target platform is produced from a program written by using an high level language, such as C, C#, CIL, and so on. More generally, a static compilation is the process of translating a program, available in a source language, into a target language, and its storing inside a file system, which makes possible later executions of it without necessitating the same compilation process anymore. Notice that static compilations do not assume the knowledge of input data of programs given as input. An example of static compilation is the translation from C to CIL described in Sect. 2.1.

As previously described, CIL programs rely on the standard library called BCL. This library is composed by several classes, which include methods; some of these

Fig. 2.1 Execution of a CIL program by using ILDJIT, which is composed by a compiler and a runtime system

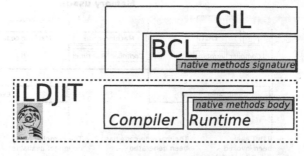

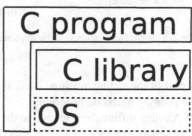

Fig. 2.2 Execution of a program written in the C language and compiled it statically

methods have their signatures described in CIL, but their bodies have to be provided by the runtime system—ILDJIT in our case. Most of these native methods are similar to the classic system calls of the underlying operating system; an example is `Platform.FileMethods.Open`, which opens a file whose name is specified as input by an object `String`. The relation between CIL programs, BCL and ILDJIT is shown in Fig. 2.1. The CIL program is translated to the machine code of the underlying platform before its execution by the compiler available inside ILDJIT. This transformation can be applied anytime (e.g., at static time or at runtime). The runtime system built inside ILDJIT is in charge to virtualize the underlying operating system by exposing the bodies of the aforementioned native methods like `Platform.FileMethods.Open`.

In order to better understand possible implementations of the static compilation scheme inside environments like CIL (similar discussion can be done for the Java environment), in the following, we describe the execution of programs written in a programming language where this scheme is usually applied: the C language.

Consider a C program for example: it is translated to machine code by a compiler like `gcc` to be later executed. The environment where these programs are executed is shown in Fig. 2.2.

The first difference between the execution of CIL and C programs is about the compiler: after C programs have been translated, the compiler does not play any role during their executions. In other words, the compiler is detached from the running produced code. On the other hand, at least CIL programs need a runtime, which is coupled with their executions; this fact suggests implementations of compilation schemes, which are usually applied to bytecode systems, where the compiler, which

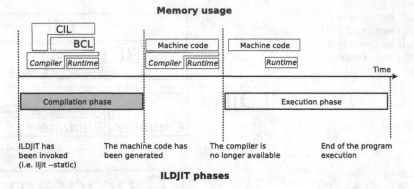

Fig. 2.3 Static compilation scheme implemented inside ILDJIT

is part of the virtual machine used, is kept in memory even after the compilation of the running bytecode program.

Another difference is related to the machine code generated: code generated from C programs interacts with the underlying operating system directly. On the other hand, code generated by the compiler built inside virtual machines, such as ILDJIT, interacts with the runtime, which can perform additional checks before redirecting the execution to the underlying operating system. This indirection can be used to improve security inside a system.

As programs that run in user space need an operating system, as CIL programs need a runtime system that provides the same kind of abstraction for the underlying platform. For this reason, ILDJIT implements the static compilation scheme in a slightly different way with respect to the aforementioned scheme. The following schemes, which are similar to the static compilation one, are provided by ILDJIT: static, ahead-of-time, partial static and partial-ahead-of-time compilations. Those schemes are introduced in the next sections.

2.2.1 Static Compilation in ILDJIT

ILDJIT implements the static compilation scheme by executing two phases in one run: the compilation and the execution phase. These phases are kept separated. This type of execution is shown in Fig. 2.3, where ILDJIT has been invoked with the parameter --static. In this compilation scheme, ILDJIT does not interchange compilation and execution of the program: first, the entire program is translated to the target machine code (e.g. Intel x86). When the machine code has been generated, and also stored in memory, ILDJIT shutdowns the compiler both to free as much memory as possible and to reduce the overall number of running threads (the compiler is multi-threaded). When only the runtime module resides in memory, the execution of the produced code can start.

In order to compile our hello world program by using the static compilation scheme, we need to execute the following command:

```
$ iljit --static ./hello_world_c.cil
Hello, world!
```

In this example, ILDJIT both produces and executes the machine code of the underlying platform of the program `hello_world_c.cil`, which prints to the terminal the string `Hello, world!`.

In order to reduce the first phase, where the machine code is generated, ILDJIT stores the optimized code in its code cache, which resides in the file system at `~/.ildjit/manfred`, where `~` refers to the home of the user (e.g. `/home/simone`). Every program has its own directory inside the code cache called with the name of its correspondent CIL file. For example, in our previous example, where we compiled and executed our hello world program, the directory `~/.ildjit/manfred/hello_world_c.cil` has been generated. The parameter of ILDJIT `--clean-code-cache` removes every code inside this code cache.

```
$ ls ~/.ildjit/manfred
hello_world_c.cil
$ iljit -clean-code-cache
$ ls ~/.ildjit/manfred
$
```

The code generated and stored inside the code cache is platform independent. ILDJIT stores its intermediate representation inside this cache instead of the final machine code. The reason is that most of the time spent by the compiler is due to the code optimizations; these optimizations are mainly performed to the intermediate representation. By storing the already optimized intermediate representation to the code cache, at the second time a program is invoked, ILDJIT loads the code from its cache (generated at the first run), it generates the machine code and it starts the execution. This time, the time spent by the compiler is negligible in usual scenarious. For example, on an Intel core i7 machine, the overall time spent by the compiler at the second invocation to generate the machine code for an entire real program is few ms.

2.2.2 Ahead-of-Time Compilation in ILDJIT

Other than the already described static compilation scheme, ILDJIT provides the ahead-of-time (AOT) compilation. The main difference between the AOT and the static compilation scheme is that in the first one, the compiler is kept in memory even

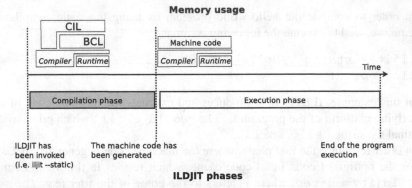

Fig. 2.4 Ahead-of-time compilation scheme implemented inside ILDJIT

after the compilation phase shown in Fig. 2.3. The resulting execution is shown in Fig. 2.4.

The AOT compilation has been introduced to compile an intermediate language, such as Java bytecode or CIL, into the target machine code before actually running it. However, recompilation of the produced code can happen at runtime in this scheme. These recompilations are typical of dynamic compilers, which exploit runtime information to produce better code. For this reason, ILDJIT keeps the compiler in memory even after the compilation phase.

2.2.3 Partial Compilations in ILDJIT

Sections 2.1 and 2.2 describes two static compilation schemes available in ILDJIT. In both cases, both the entire program and everything it is linked with are translated to the ILDJIT intermediate representation (IR) first and to the machine code later. Consider for example our hello world program, `hello_world_c.cil`. In this case, every method defined either inside the `hello_world_c.cil` file or inside the entire BCL is compiled.

On top of these two schemes, ILDJIT provides a partial compilation option, `-P1`, which can be used for both ones. When this option is specified, ILDJIT applies the chosen compilation scheme only to those methods effectively executed by a previous run of the program. This type of partial compilation is structured in three phases: first, we need to clear the code cache.

```
$ iljit -clean-code-cache
```

Second, the program is executed to keep track of which methods are needed.

```
$ ls ~/. ildjit/manfred
$ iljit -P1 ./hello_world_c.cil
Hello, world!
```

```
$ ls ~/. ildjit/manfred
hello_world_c.cil
```

Finally, the chosen compilation scheme is applied constraining it to the methods previously executed.

```
$ iljit -P1--static ./hello_world_c.cil
Hello, world!
$ ls ~/. ildjit/manfred
hello_world_c.cil
```

Later executions of the program do not need the -P1 option anymore because the code has been generated already. Hence

```
$ iljit --static ./hello_world_c.cil
Hello, world!
or
$ iljit-aot ./hello_world_c.cil
Hello, world!
```

Notice that even if the second phase does not produce any code, after its execution, a code cache entry for the considered program has been created. Information inside the code cache at that stage includes profiling data only. Hence, no code is included. By looking inside the cache, we can see a file called profile.ir.

```
$ iljit --clean-code-cache
$ iljit -P1 ./hello_world_c.cil
Hello, world!
$ ls ~/. ildjit/manfred
hello_world_c.cil
$ ls ~/. ildjit/manfred/hello_world_c.cil/*.ir
profile.ir
```

On the other hand, after the third phase, the same code cache entry of the considered program includes code effectively. Hence, the third phase replaces the profile data with the generated code.

```
$ ls ~/. ildjit/manfred/hello_world_c.cil/*.ir
profile.ir
$ iljit -P1 --static ./hello_world_c.cil
Hello, world!
$ ls ~/. ildjit/manfred/hello_world_c.cil/*.ir
methods.ir
```

The file methods.ir contains the code of the methods specified inside the file profile.ir.

Fig. 2.5 IR produced inside one system and exploited by another one

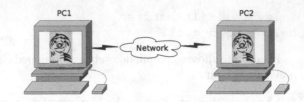

2.2.4 Cached Code

As previously described, the code stored inside the code cache of ILDJIT (i.e., ~/. ildjit/manfred) contains the IR representation of the program. By default, ILDJIT stores platform independent code inside this cache only (this behavior can be changed by customizing the framework as described in Chap. 6). Since the cached code is platform independent, we can exploit it on different systems where either the underlying operating system or the platform can differs with respect to the one used to produce that code.

Consider for example the scenarios described by Fig. 2.5 where two computers are involved: PC1 and PC2. The first one, PC1, has a Windows operating system installed on top of an Intel x86 processor. On the other hand, the second one, PC2, has Linux installed on top of an ARM processor. The code is first generated on PC1.

```
PC1 $ iljit --static hello_world_c.cil
Hello, world!
```

Then, the code cache is transfered from PC1 to PC2.

```
PC1 $ rcp -r ~/. ildjit/manfred/hello_world_c.cil
      PC1: ~/. ildjit/manfred/
```

Hence, ILDJIT installed on PC2 can exploit the code produced by PC1.

```
PC2 $ iljit --static hello_world_c.cil
Hello, world!
```

Thanks to this platform independent property of the produced IR code, CIL programs can be compiled once and used inside every system ILDJIT has been installed into, no matter which system produced that code.

2.3 Dynamic Compilation

Software portability suggests the generation of portable intermediate binary code, that remains independent from the specific hardware architecture and is executed by a software layer called *virtual machine (VM)* [9]. A virtual machine provides an interface to an abstract computing machine that accepts the intermediate binary code as its native language; in this way, the virtualization of the instruction set architecture (ISA) is performed. The dynamic compilation approach was introduced to overcome the slowness of the first generation of virtual machines, where the execution of bytecode programs was entirely interpreted: they interpreted bytecode rather than first compiling it to machine code and then executing the so produced code. This approach, of course, did not offer the best possible performance, as the system spent more time executing the interpreter than the program it was supposed to be running.

ILDJIT provides two different dynamic compilation schemes: the just-in-time (JIT) [9] and the dynamic-look-ahead (DLA) [2] one. In both cases, the code cache is not used. The second one, the DLA compilation, is a natural evolution of the JIT compilation specifically designed for the multicore era. These schemes interchange the compilation and the execution of the program leading to an interleaving of the corresponding phases shown in Fig. 2.3.

The code produced by dynamic compilers can be different with respect to the one produced by static compilers described in Sect. 2.2. The reasons are the following: first the compilation performed at runtime should be as fast as possible in order to reduce its overhead at runtime. Hence, the dynamic compiler cannot spend too much time to optimize the code. Second, the compilation performed at runtime can exploit runtime information, such as values of method parameters, not available at static time.

2.3.1 Just-in-Time Compilation

Strictly defined, a JIT compiler translates bytecode into machine code, before its execution, in a lazy fashion: the JIT compiles a code path only when it knows that code path is about to be executed (hence the name, just-in-time compilation). This approach allows the program to start up more quickly, as a lengthy compilation phase is not needed before execution beginning. Figure 2.6 shows the execution of ILDJIT by using this scheme. This figure shows that the machine code is generated during the entire execution of the program by interleaving execution and compilation phases. Hence, the memory used to store the produced code grows as the execution of the program proceeds. Several approaches have been proposed in literature [9] to constrain this memory growing effect by discarding code produced in the past which is likely to be not useful in the near future. By default, ILDJIT does not constrain this growing effect. However, as described in Chap. 6, ILDJIT can be customized to change this behavior.

The JIT compiler is the default compilation scheme used by ILDJIT. Hence, we do not need additional options to use it.

```
$ iljit hello_world_c.cil
Hello, world!
```

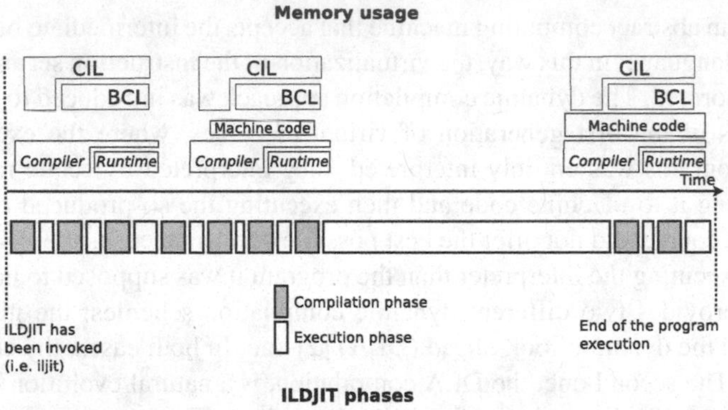

Memory usage

Fig. 2.6 Just-in-time compilation scheme implemented inside ILDJIT

The JIT approach seems promising comparing it to the bytecode interpretation solution, but it presents some drawbacks: JIT compilation removes the overhead due to the interpretation at the expense of some additional startup cost, and the level of code optimization is mediocre. To avoid a significant startup penalty for portable applications, the JIT compiler has to be fast, which means that it cannot spend much time in optimization. The next section describes an evolution of this scheme, called Dynamic Look-Ahead compilation [10], which exploits the parallelism available in multicore architectures to both improve the quality of the code and to reduce the compilation time perceived by the execution of the program.

2.3.2 Dynamic Look-Ahead Compilation

Dynamically compiled code can achieve large speedups, especially in the long run, since the execution of a native method is an order of magnitude faster than that of an interpreted one. However, the performance of a JIT-based dynamic compiler is still lower than that of native code produced by static compilation schemes like the AOT one. The loss of performance is due to both compilation overhead, often called *startup time*, and to the poor quality of the generated code, since the startup time minimization prevents the aggressive and costly optimizations usually performed by static compilers.

Nowadays, multi-core technology has become the predominant technology in both desktop and embedded domains. This type of hardware architecture is a way to provide more computational power without relying on the reduction of the clock cycle, which is becoming increasingly difficult due to technology limitations. For this reason, dynamic look-ahead (DLA) compilers exploit multiprocessor environments by introducing compiler threads, which can dynamically compile bytecode portions in advance, in parallel with the application execution. Strictly defined, a DLA compiler translates and optimizes bytecode looking ahead of the execution

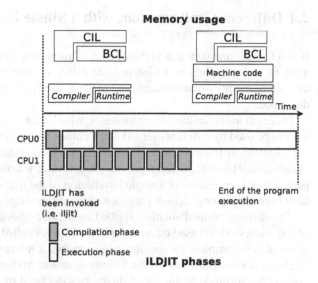

Fig. 2.7 Dynamic look-ahead compilation scheme implemented inside ILDJIT

in order to both anticipate the compilation before the execution asks for it, and to produce optimized code.

DLA compilers are based on a software pipeline architecture for compilation, optimization and execution tasks. While a processor is executing a method, compilation threads (running on other processors) *look ahead* into the call graph, detecting methods that have good chances to be executed in the near future. Moreover, they guess whether a method is a *hot spot* [9] (code often executed) or not, and apply aggressive optimizations accordingly. In the best case, there is no compilation overhead, because compilation fully overlaps with execution and methods are already compiled when they are invoked. Moreover, optimizations are fully exploited to provide high quality code.

Figure 2.7 shows a typical execution of a DLA compiler. The main difference with respect to JIT compilers is that DLA compilers can translate more code than the JIT ones (because it compiles in advance methods by guessing where the execution is going). Moreover, the produced code is optimized already before its first execution.

In order to use the DLA compiler available in ILDJIT, the option –dla is provided.

```
$ iljit --dla hello_world_c.cil
Hello, world!
```

By default, ILDJIT exploits every core provided by the underlying platform whenever the DLA compiler is used and there is a peak in term of methods to compile to run the application.

2.4 Different Configurations with a Single Installation

ILDJIT is a framework that includes a set of modules, which compose its core, and a set of external plugins, which provide different type of translations, code optimizations, memory managements and policies used by various compilers previously described.

Different users can have different needs, which means that different sets of plugins have to be used by different users. ILDJIT comes with a default set of plugins, which are installed in the system, and therefore, they are shared between users of that installation. However, ILDJIT provides a solution, following described, of having personal customizations of a single installation of the framework. This can be useful both to override some default plugins and to add new ones.

The aforementioned solution applied to ILDJIT about personal customizations of the framework is based on environment variables called `ILDJIT_X_PLUGINS`, where X is the name of the specific extension that it refers to. At boost time, ILDJIT loads these customizations in the following order: first, it loads the plugins in the same order specified by the list of directories declared by the environemnt variable `ILDJIT_X_PLUGINS`. Finally, it loads plugins from the directory where it has been installed. Consider for example the following list of directories:

```
$ echo $ ILDJIT_X_PLUGINS
/home/simone/first:/home/simone/second
```

Assuming that ILDJIT is installed inside the default directory, which is `/usr/local`, then plugins are loaded and used in the following order: `/home/simone/first`, `/home/simone/second`, `/usr/local/lib/iljit/optim-izers`. Assuming that we have a task, like dead code elimination, which is provided by two different plugins: one provided by the default installation and one installed in `/home/simone/first`. In this case, by having the directories specified as for the previous variable `ILDJIT_X_PLUGINS`, ILDJIT will use the plugin installed in `/home/simone/first`. On the other hand, if we change the value of the variable `ILDJIT_X_PLUGINS` as following:

```
$ export ILDJIT_X_PLUGINS=/home/simone/second
```

then the plugin provided by the default installation will be used. In order to provide this behavior, ILDJIT links at runtime plugins found in the system, which provide tasks not provided by other plugins that it is not already linked with.

Consider a scenario where there are three users: `alex`, `bob` and `tom`. Consider also that ILDJIT has been installed inside the default directory and that these three users share the same system (or they share the file system at least). Imagine that `alex` and `bob` need to customize ILDJIT with their own plugins. Moreover, `tom` needs both to customize ILDJIT with his own plugins and to use bob's plugins. In this case, alex needs to set the aforementioned variable as following:

```
$ export ILDJIT_X_PLUGINS=/home/alex/my_plugins
```

On the other hand, bob needs to set it as following:

```
$ export ILDJIT_X_PLUGINS=/home/bob/my_plugins
```

Finally, tom needs to set the variable to point to the following two directories:

```
$ export ILDJIT_X_PLUGINS=/home/tom/my_plugins:
/home/bob/my_plugins
```

Notice that tom needs to have read access to the bob's directory in order to use his plugins.

References

1. Campanoni, S., Agosta, G., Crespi-Reghizzi S., Biagio A.D.: A highly flexible, parallel virtual machine: design and experience of ILDJIT. In: Software: Practice and Experience, pp. 177–207 Wiley (2010)
2. ECMA ECMA-335: common language infrastructure (CLI). http://www.ecma-international. org/publications/files/ECMA-ST/Ecma-335 pdf (2010). Cited 11 June 2011
3. ISO (1999). ISO C Standard 1999
4. ISO (2003). ISO/IEC 14882:2003
5. Gosling, J., Bill, J., Steele, G., Bracha, G.: The Java Language Specification. 3rd edn. Addison-Wesley (2005)
6. ECMA ECMA-334: C# Language Specification. http://www.ecma-international.org/ publications/files/ECMA-ST/Ecma-334.pdf (2006). Cited 11 June 2011
7. Costa, R., Ornstein A.C., Rohou, E. GCC4CLI. http://gcc.gnu.org/projects/cli.html (2010). Cited 11 June 2011
8. de Icaza, M., Molaro, P., Mono, D.M. http://www.mono-project.com (2011).Cited 11 June 2011
9. Smith, J., Nair R.: Virtual Machines: versatile platforms for systems and processes. In: The Morgan Kaufmann Series in Computer Architecture and Design, Morgan Kaufmann Publishers (2005)
10. Campanoni, S., Sykora M., Agosta, G., Crespi-Reghizzi S.: Dynamic look ahead compilation: a technique to hide JIT compilation latencies in multicore environment. International conference on compiler construction, pp. 220–235 (2009)

Chapter 3
Platform Independent Extensions of the Framework

Abstract Extensions of the compilation framework Intermediate Language Distributed Just in Time (ILDJIT) can be provided. In order to use these extensions on any platform where the framework is able to run on, ILDJIT provides both data types and a platform independent API. The developer should use them instead of using their correspondent platform specific ones. This chapter describes both these data types and this platform independent API.

Keywords Compilation framework extensions · Platform independent code · Platform Independent data types · Platform independent API · System calls

Intermediate Language Distributed Just in Time (ILDJIT) allows its users to extend the framework, by means of new external plugins, to better fit their specific needs. However, since these extensions can be implemented using the C language, the users are in charge to implement their own plugins in order to be platform independent.

In order to help users to write platform independent code, ILDJIT provides both a set of data types that are platform independent and an API that abstracts the underlying operating system. As shown in Fig. 3.1, in order to maximize the platform independent code inside the entire system, these abstractions compose the lowest layer of both the framework and its extensions. The framework maps both these data types and the functions that compose the platform independent API to the correspondent ones of the underlying platform at the time ILDJIT is installed inside the system.

3.1 Platform Independent Data Types

Data types that are independent from the underlying platform have names that started with the prefix JIT. For example, a 32 bit unsigned integer value, which is called my_variable, has to be declared inside the code as following:

```
JITUINT32 my_variable;
```

Fig. 3.1 Platform
independent API used by
both the framework and
ILDJIT extensions

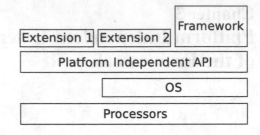

Both integer variables, either signed or unsigned, of fixed number of bits from 8 to 64 (e.g. JITUINT64) and variables with a data type that depends on the underlying platform can be declared. For example, the data type of signed integer values with number of bits that depends on the underlying platform is JITNINT (i.e., JIT Native INTeger). Variables declared to have this type can store 32 (64) bits values for 32 (64) bit processors. Moreover, the unsigned version of JITNINT, which is JITNUINT (JIT Unsigned Native INTeger), is available as well.

Floating point values can be used by declaring them with the type JITFLOAT32, JITFLOAT64 or JITNFLOAT; their names self-describe their semantics.

Special values of the introduced data types are provided by the framework to be platform independent. They are the boundary of the range of possible values that can be stored by their correspondent data types. For example, JITMAXINT8 (JITMININT8) corresponds to the highest (lowest) value that can be stored inside a variable of type JITINT8. These couple of values are available for every data type.

Both data types and their special values are defined inside the file jitsystem.h.

3.2 Platform Independent API

ILDJIT is a program that runs on top of an operating system; therefore, users that want to extend this framework can rely on system calls provided by the underlying operating system. Since different operating systems have different system calls, ILDJIT provides a platform independent API, which abstracts from the specific system calls provided by the actual operating system where the framework is running on. Users that want to write platform independent extensions of this framework have to use this API instead of calling the underlying operating system directly.

The platform independent API is defined inside the file platform_API.h, which includes both classic system calls and higher functions, such as locking mutexes. Functions that compose this API have names that start with the prefix PLATFORM. Examples of these functions are the following ones:

```
JITNINT PLATFORM_broadcastCondVar (
    pthread_cond_t *arg1);
JITNINT PLATFORM_destroyCondVar (
    pthread_cond_t *arg1);
```

```
JITNINT PLATFORM_closeDir(
  DIR *arg1);
```

The platform independent API includes functions that handle threads, such as PLATFORM_broadcastCondVar that unblocks all threads currently blocked on the condition variable given as input, input/output, such as PLATFORM_closeDir that closes a directory previously opened and finally they interact with the underlying operating system to get platform information, such as the name of the host.

Chapter 4
Compiling with Optimization

Abstract ILDJIT translates the CIL program given as input to its intermediate representation (IR). Several code optimization algorithms can be applied to IR code before producing the correspondent machine code. This chapter starts by describing the general idea behind code optimization algorithms in order to better describe how they can be applied inside the ILDJIT compilation framework, which organizes them in *optimization levels*.

Keywords Code optimizations · Code optimization levels · Compilation framework extensions

The generation of machine code of a target platform from CIL bytecode given as input to ILDJIT [1] can be performed in several ways. A naive approach for this task, where the machine code is generated straight from the input bytecode, does not generate the code that leads to the best performance at runtime. Instead, by applying a set of algorithms to the program, called code optimizations, ILDJIT is able to produce code optimized for a given metric, such as performance, memory used or power.

After giving some examples of code optimizations to show their potentiality, this chapter introduces how code optimizations are organized in ILDJIT by defining its *optimization levels*. Optimizations declared in these levels can be changed by using options of ILDJIT in order to choose subsets of those. Finally, this chapter describes how to redefine the optimization levels by adding new customizations to the framework by means of new external plugins.

4.1 Code Optimizations

Code optimization algorithms can be effective on improving metrics like performance, memory used or power consumed by the produced code due to several reasons including redundancy that exists inside the program, computations that can

S. Campanoni, *Guide to ILDJIT*, SpringerBriefs in Computer Science,
DOI: 10.1007/978-1-4471-2194-7_4, © Simone Campanoni 2011

be performed at compile time rather than at runtime or better exploitation of the underlying hardware resources. The redundancy can come straight from the developer or it can be highlighted by a previous code optimization applied to the code.

For example, consider the following C code:

```
a = 2 ;
b = a ;
c = b * 3 ;
c = c + 1 ;
d = b * 3 ;
return c + d;
```

We can notice that the expression b*3 is computed twice inside the code, and the second one is redundant because both computations lead to the same result during every possible executions of that piece of code. Hence, the code can be optimized to remove away one multiplication from it, which produces the following code:

```
a = 2;
b = a ;
c = b * 3 ;
d = c ;
c = c + 1 ;
return c + d;
```

The previous transformation could be safely applied to the initial program because the transformed code has the same *semantic* of the original one. Two programs are considered *semantically equivalent* if they produce the same effects to the user of those programs. Deeper discussions about code optimizations can be found in [2] and in [1]. The previously code optimization applied is called *common sub-expressions elimination*.

In order to be able to later apply another type of optimization called *constant folding*, the assignment b=a is safely substituted by b=2 producing the following code:

```
a = 2 ;
b = 2 ;
c = b * 3;
d = c ;
c = c + 1 ;
return c + d;
```

We can apply another substitution of b used inside the multiplication instruction, which produces the following code:

```
a = 2 ;
b = 2 ;
c = 2 * 3 ;
d = c ;
c = c + 1 ;
return c + d;
```

Looking at the produced code, we can make two observations: the variables a and b are not used anymore, hence their assignments are unnecessary, or, in other words, are dead code. Second, the computation of the multiplication specified inside the code can be performed at compile time; there is no need to compute it at runtime, which would lead to use resources unnecessary during the execution of the program. Applying both the *dead code elimination* and the *constant folding* algorithms [2], the following code is produced:

```
c = 6 ;
d = c ;
c = c + 1;
return c + d;
```

By applying for the second time the same set of code optimization algorithms we applied so far, we produce the following final code:

```
return 13 ;
```

By comparing the optimized code and the original one, we can conclude saying that the time spent by these semantically equivalent programs is quite different at runtime: the optimized code will be executed in fewer clock cycles compared to the original one.

Several algorithms to optimize the code have been proposed in literature. Some of them do not exploit specific details of the underlying platform (i.e., they are platform independent, such as constant folding) and some of them use these details. In ILDJIT, platform dependent code optimizations are invoked only after that the platform independent ones have been applied to the code.

4.2 Optimization Levels

ILDJIT organizes code optimization algorithms in two symmetric group of levels. Code optimizations that use details of the underlying platform (i.e., platform dependent code optimizations) are grouped together. On the other hand, platform independent code optimizations belong to the second group.

Each group of levels is composed by a set of those defined with a number starting from 0 and two levels called *AOT* and *Post-AOT*. The execution model of ILDJIT is the following: when a method needs to be compiled (which methods are compiled depends on the compilation scheme used; see Chap. 2), it is translated to the ILDJIT

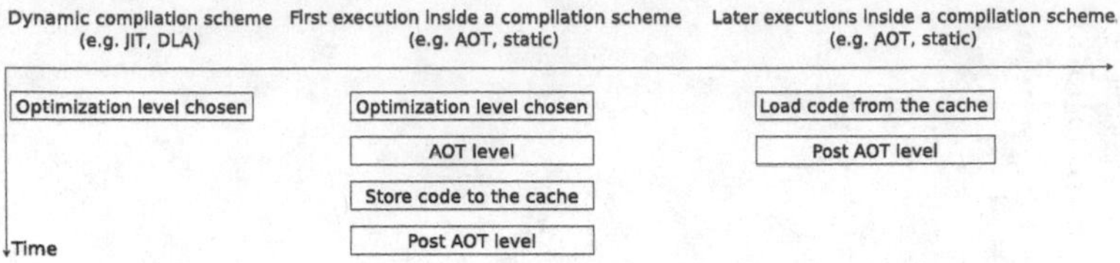

Dynamic compilation scheme (e.g. JIT, DLA)	First execution inside a compilation scheme (e.g. AOT, static)	Later executions inside a compilation scheme (e.g. AOT, static)
Optimization level chosen	Optimization level chosen	Load code from the cache
	AOT level	Post AOT level
	Store code to the cache	
↓Time	Post AOT level	

Fig. 4.1 Optimization levels applied by different compilation schemes

internal representation (IR). Optimizations defined at the chosen optimization level (e.g. 2) are applied to the IR code; if a static compilation scheme is chosen (i.e., static, AOT, partial static, partial AOT compilations), then first the optimizations defined at level AOT and then the ones defined at level Post-AOT are applied to the code. After having applied these optimizations, the IR code is finally generated to the target machine code (e.g., Intel x86).

For example, let us assume that the first optimization level defines only the constant folding code optimization. Let us assume also that both the AOT level defines the constant propagation optimization and the Post-AOT level defines the copy propagation optimization [2]. In this case, the following invocation of ILDJIT leads to apply the following optimizations in the following order: constant folding, constant propagation and copy propagation.

```
$iljit-O1 --aot hello_world_c.cil
Hello, world!
```

The same set of optimizations are applied in the same order by the following execution of ILDJIT:

```
$iljit -O1 --static hello_world_c.cil
Hello, world!
```

On the other hand, the following invocation of ILDJIT leads to apply only the constant folding optimization:

```
$iljit -O1 hello_world_c.cil
Hello, world!
```

In conclusion, the numbered optimization levels are always applied to produce the executed code; on the other hand, AOT and Post-AOT are applied only when static compilation schemes are used. Figure 4.1 shows how these levels are applied to the code inside the available compilation schemes.

The difference between the AOT and Post-AOT level is due to the previosuly introduced code cache: the first time a program is executed by using a static compilation scheme, first the chosen numbered optimization level (e.g., O1) and then the AOT optimization level is applied to the code. After these two levels have been applied to the code, the generated IR code is stored inside the code cache of ILDJIT. Before starting the code translation to the target machine code, the Post-AOT optimization level is applied to the IR code (which is the one stored inside the code cache). Notice that the IR code generated by the Post-AOT level is not stored anywhere by default (this behaviour can be changed by providing an external plugin as described

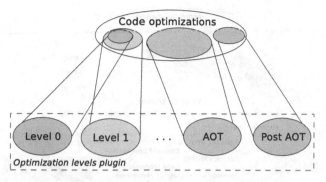

Fig. 4.2 Definition of the optimization levels by means of the optimization levels plugin

in Sect. 4.4). At the second, or later, execution of a program, ILDJIT loads its IR code from the code cache, it applies the Post-AOT optimization level only (other optimization levels have already applied to the code loaded from the code cache, and therefore, there is no need to apply them again) and it generates the target machine code. Hence, the Post-AOT level is always applied to the code when a static compilation scheme is used, no matter if the code was already generated in the past or not. On the other hand, other optimization levels are applied to the code either when the code is generated and stored to the cache (during the first execution of programs) or a dynamic compilation scheme is used.

As shown in Fig. 4.2, the definition of each level (i.e., which optimizations are used in which levels) is provided by the *optimization levels* external plugin. In this way, ILDJIT allows the user to redefine these levels.

This design choice is due to the fact that both the set of optimizations to apply to the code and how many times a given optimization would be applied to the code is domain specific. For example, consider a scenario where there is a single program running on a platform where the instruction cache is shared across 2 cores. In this case, the loop unrolling algorithm (a loop is unrolled in order to both reduce the number of executed branches and apply further optimizations to a larger loop body) [2] can speedup the execution. Hence, a good definition of the optimization levels should include this algorithm. On the other hand, let us assume another scenario where two programs are running at the same time. In this case, a loop unrolling should be used more carefully (e.g., by unrolling the loop less times) because it can slowdown the execution of the second program. The reason is that by unrolling the first program loop can lead to an excessive use of the instruction cache, which now contains only the unrolled loop body, leaving almost no cache for the second program. In this case, the execution of the second program would lead to additional instruction cache misses, which will slowdown its execution. Notice that the platform did not change in these two cases, only the scenario did.

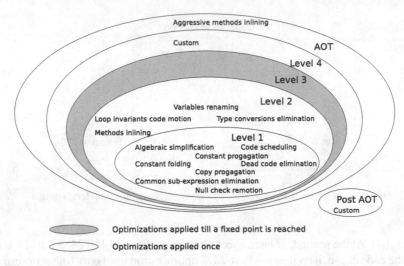

Fig. 4.3 Definition of the optimization levels by means of the default optimization levels plugin

4.2.1 Default Optimization Levels

ILDJIT comes with a default optimization levels plugin, which defines the optimization levels as shown in Fig. 4.3. As described in Sect. 4.4, this plugin can be replaced by providing a new version of it, which allows to the user to define his or her own optimizations levels.

Every optimization level includes the lower ones. For example, code optimizations defined inside level 2 are included in level 3, and so on. Moreover, this plugin defines these levels independently from the compilation scheme used: the first optimization level is the same for AOT, static, JIT or DLA compilers. As already mentioned, this behavior can be changed by providing a new optimization levels plugin, which can take into account the compilation scheme used, and therefore, it can define the optimization levels accordingly.

Independently on the definition of optimization levels, ILDJIT can be called to force the compiler to apply the specified level to every compiled method. For example, the following invocation of ILDJIT applies every code optimization defined either at level 0 or at level 1 to every method executed by the available JIT compiler:

```
$iljit -O1 hello_world_c.cil
Hello, world!
```

Moreover, the following execution of ILDJIT applies every code optimization defined either at level 0 or at level 1 to every method executed by the available AOT compiler:

```
$iljit -O1 --aot hello_world_c.cil
Hello, world!
```

As we can notice, the compilation scheme to use and the optimization level to apply are orthogonal concepts whenever the default installation of ILDJIT is used.

4.3 Enable and Disable Optimizations

Independently from the definition of the optimization levels, ILDJIT provides the possibility of enabling, or disabling, a set of code optimization algorithms specified as input. The specification of the code optimizations to consider is given by the list of their correspondent names separated by commas. For example, the list cse,cfold corresponds to the common sub-expression elimination and constant folding code optimizations. For the entire list of code optimizations available in ILDJIT, type iljit as following:

```
$ iljit --optimizations
The following optimizations are available:
    Constant folding: cfold
    Constant propagation: consprop
    Copy propagation: copyprop
    Common sub-expressions elimination: cse
    Dead code elimination: deadce
    Instruction scheduling: sched
    Remove useless checks of null pointers: nullcheck
    Algebraic simplification: algebraic
    Variables renaming: variablesrename
    Methods inlining: methodinline
    Native methods inlining: nativemethodinline
    Conversion merging: convmerging
    Escapes elimination: escapes
    Custom: custom
```

Next sections describe how to either disable or enable optimization algorithms in ILDJIT. The correspondent options are --disable-optimizations and --enable-optimizations respectively. These two options cannot be used together; as later described, there is no need to do it.

4.3.1 Disabling Optimizations

The disabling option, --disable-optimizations, removes the specified list of optimizations from the chosen optimization level. This option can be applied to every optimization level inside every compilation scheme (e.g. AOT, JIT, etc ldots).

For example, assuming the optimization level O1 being composed by the optimizations cfold, cse and escapes, the following command optimizes the code by applying the optimization escapes only:

```
$iljit -O1 --disable-optimizations=cfold,cse
   hello_world_c.cil
 Hello, world!
```

The following invocation of ILDJIT optimizes the executed methods by applying every optimization defined at level 2 without using the common sub-expression elimination optimization:

```
$iljit -O2--disable-optimizations=cse
  hello_world_c.cil
Hello, world!
```

Hence, the --disable-optimizations option is equivalent to the minus set operation between the optimizations defined inside the chosen level and the specified list of optimizations (i.e., {*Level*2} -{*cse*}). Notice that if the common subexpression elimination is not included to the optimization level 2, the previous execution would be equal to the following one:

```
iljit -O2 hello_world_c.cil
$Hello, world!
```

4.3.2 Enabling Optimizations

The enabling option, --enable-optimizations, applies to the code only the optimizations that are both defined inside the chosen level and defined by the given list of the aforementioned option.

For example, assuming the optimization level one be composed by the optimizations cfold, cse and escapes, the following command optimizes the code by applying the optimization escapes only:

```
$iljit -O1 --enable-optimizations=escapes
  hello_world_c.cil
Hello, world!
```

The following invocation of ILDJIT optimizes the executed methods by applying the common sub-expression elimination optimization only if it has been included inside the second optimization level:

```
$iljit -O2 --enable-optimizations=cse
  hello_world_c.cil
Hello, world!
```

As highlighted by the previous examples, the --enable-optimizations option is equivalent to the set intersection operation between the optimizations defined inside the chosen level and the specified list of optimizations (i.e., {*Level*2} ∩ {*cse*}).

4.4 Customizing Optimization Levels

Optimization levels can be defined by means of an *optimization levels* plugin. Plugins are external libraries installed independently inside the system. In order to be able to compile plugins, the necessary headers, which are installed with the ILDJIT installation, have to be installed inside the system.

ILDJIT provides a dummy example for this type of plugin called *dummy optimiza-tion levels*. The interface between this type of plugin and ILDJIT is the following:

```
/* ir_optimization_levels.h */
typedef struct {
  JITUINT32 (*optimizeMethodAtLevel)(
    ir_optimizer_t *lib,
    ir_method_t *method,
    JITUINT32 optimizationLevel,
    XanVar *status);
  JITUINT32 (*optimizeMethodAtAOTLevel)(
    ir_optimizer_t *lib,
    ir_method_t *entryPointMethod,
    XanVar *status);
  JITUINT32 (*optimizeMethodAtPostAOTLevel)(
    ir_optimizer_t *lib,
    ir_method_t *entryPointMethod,
    XanVar *status);
} ir_optimization_levels_t;
```

The structure ir_optimization_levels_t provides three functions that every optimization levels plugin has to provide. Optimization levels are described by providing the body of these three functions described in the next sections.

The API between an optimization levels plugin and ILDJIT is composed by both the already introduced functions that these plugins have to implement and a set of functions provided by ILDJIT that these plugins can rely on. The following sections describe each of them.

4.4.1 Optimization Levels API

As previously described, each optimization levels plugin has to implement the follow-ing functions, which defines the optimization levels to use: optimizeMethodAt Level, optimizeMethodAtAOTLevel and optimizeMethodAtPost AOTLevel. The first one, optimizeMethodAtLevel, defines the numbered optimization levels; the last two define the AOT and Post AOT level respectively. The definition of a level is provided by the invocations of the code optimization algorithms performed inside the correspondent function.

For example, the following code defines the AOT level as composed by the constant propagation code optimization only:

```
JITUINT32 (*optimizeMethodAtAOTLevel) (
    ir_optimizer_t *lib,
    ir_method_t *method,
    XanVar *status){
```

```
IROPTIMIZER_callMethodOptimization(
  lib,
  method,
  CONSTANT_PROPAGATION);
}
```

Notice that the definition of a level is a C function, which means that can be described by means of any algorithm. For example, we can define a level as composed by the constant propagation applied three times as the following example shows:

```
JITUINT32 (*optimizeMethodAtAOTLevel) (
    ir_optimizer_t *lib,
    ir_method_t *method,
    XanVar *status){
int c;
for (c = 0; c < 3; c++){
  IROPTIMIZER_callMethodOptimization(
    lib,
    method,
    CONSTANT_PROPAGATION);
  }
}
```

The functions that each plugin has to provide include the parameter status, which is a variable that can be used to receive requests from ILDJIT inside the plugin. This variable can assume two values: JOB_START and JOB_END; the first value, JOB_START, means that the plugin can continue to optimize the code by calling the necessary code optimization algorithms. On the other hand, the value JOB_END means that the plugin should stop to optimize the code and it should return the execution to ILDJIT as soon as possible. In this way, ILDJIT can ask the plugin to stop to optimize the code, which is a request often used inside the DLA compilation scheme, where a compilation of a method can suddenly become critical (the execution of the code is waiting for it) [2].

This variable can be read inside the optimization levels plugin by calling the function read as following:

```
JITUINT32 (*optimizeMethodAtPostAOTLevel) (
    ir_optimizer_t *lib,
    ir_method_t *method,
    XanVar *status){
JITBOOLEAN valueRead;
...
valueRead=(JITBOOLEAN)(JITNUINT)status->read(status);
if (valueRead == JOB_END) return JOB_START;
...
}
```

Each of the three functions that the plugin has to implement can return two values only: JOB_START and JOB_END. These values have the following semantic: JOB_END means that the plugin was able to optimize the code till completion. On the other hand, JOB_START means that the plugin started to optimize the code, but it has received a request to interrupt the optimization of that code. Hence, the code was not optimized as it was supposed to be.

4.4.2 Available Functions

The optimization levels plugin can use the functions available inside the following headers: ir_optimizer.h and ir_method.h. The first ILDJIT header, ir_optimizer.h, includes the following function, which can be used to call a given code optimization algorithm (such as constant folding):

```
void IROPTIMIZER_callMethodOptimization (
    ir_optimizer_t *lib,
    ir_method_t *method,
    JITUINT64 optimizationKind);
```

An example of call to this function is the following:

```
IROPTIMIZER_callMethodOptimization(
    lib,
    method,
    COPY_PROPAGATION);
```

From the previous example, we can notice that, in order to call a code optimization algorithm, an identificator of the algorithm is used (e.g. COPY_PROPAGATION). The header ir_optimizer.h includes the full list of available identificators of code optimization algorithms.

Optimization levels plugins can use the available functions defined inside the header ir_method.h, which defines the *IR API*. Inside this header there are more than three hundred functions, which can be used to look inside the code that composes a method. An example is the following one, which checks the number of instructions that compose a method:

```
JITUINT32 IRMETHOD_getInstructionsNumber (
    ir_method_t *method);
```

With this simple function, we can define the AOT optimization level as following, where we apply the constant propagation algorithm to the code only if the method has more than 1000 instructions:

```
JITUINT32 (*optimizeMethodAtAOTLevel) (
    ir_optimizer_t *lib,
    ir_method_t *method,
    XanVar *status){
```

```
if (IRMETHOD_getInstructionsNumber(method) > 1000){
  IROPTIMIZER_callMethodOptimization(
  lib,
  method,
  CONSTANT_PROPAGATION);
  }
}
```

4.4.3 Example of Optimization Levels Plugin

Armed with both the IR and the Optimizations APIs, we provide a simple example of optimization levels plugin. The following code is a simplified version of the one available inside the default ILDJIT installation.

First we define the AOT and Post AOT levels as empty.

```
JITUINT32 (*optimizeMethodAtAOTLevel)(
    ir_optimizer_t *lib,
    ir_method_t *entryPointMethod,
    XanVar *status){
return JOB_END;
}
JITUINT32 (*optimizeMethodAtPostAOTLevel)(
    ir_optimizer_t *lib,
    ir_method_t *method,
    JITUINT32 optimizationLevel,
    XanVar *status){
return JOB_END;
}
```

Now we define the numbered optimization levels, where every level includes the lower ones.

```
JITUINT32 (*optimizeMethodAtLevel)(
    ir_method_t *method,
    JITUINT32 optimizationLevel,
    XanVar *status){
JITBOOLEAN status = JOB_END;
switch(optimizationLevel){
  case 3:
    IROPTIMIZER_callMethodOptimization(
      lib, method,
      CONSTANT_PROPAGATION);
  case 2:
    status=(JITBOOLEAN)(JITNUINT)status->read(status);
```

```
    if (status == JOB_END) {
      status = JOB_START; break;
    }
    IROPTIMIZER_callMethodOptimization(
      lib, method,
      COPY_PROPAGATION);
  case 1:
      status=(JITBOOLEAN)(JITNUINT)status-> read(status);
      if (status == JOB_END) {
        status = JOB_START; break;
      }
      IROPTIMIZER_callMethodOptimization(
        lib, method,
        DEADCODE_ELIMINATION);
        break;
  }
    return status;
}
```

Notice that after every call to a code optimization algorithm, we check if the optimization should be stopped. In this case, the execution returns to ILDJIT as soon as possible. Moreover, the optimization levels plugin is not aware on where the code that implements a given code optimization algorithm is; it only requests which code optimization algorithms wants to apply to a given method. On the other hand, ILDJIT is in charge to forward the execution to the right module of the framework, which is able to perform the requested algorithm. In other words, the code optimization algorithm and its actual implementation are decoupled.

4.4.4 Installing Optimization Levels Plugins

Previous sections described how to choose subset of optimizations defined by a given optimization levels plugin installed inside the system. Also, they describe how to define new optimization levels from scratch by means of a new plugin. Here, we describe how to compile and install this new plugin inside the system.

Both the compilation and installation of a new plugin, next described, follow the standard process of Linux like packages. In order to compile a new plugin, we need to go in the parent directory of the plugin. Hence,

```
$ ls
...
src
...
```

The plugin needs to be first configured by running the following script:

```
$ ./configure
checking for a BSD-compatible install...
checking whether build environment is sane...
checking for a thread-safe mkdir -p...
...
```

Now that the plugin has been configured, we can compile it as following:

```
$ make
Making all in src
make[1]: Entering directory ...
make all-am
make[2]: Entering directory
...
```

It is time to install it inside the system by typing the following command:

```
$ make install
aking install in src
make[1]: Entering directory ...
make[2]: Entering directory
...
```

Assuming that both the compilation and installation succeed (hence, the implementation of the new plugin has no compilation error inside), we need to tell to ILDJIT both where it has been installed the new plugin and which plugin the framework should use. As in Sect. 2.4, the solution is based on an environment variable called ILDJIT_OPTIMIZATION_LEVELS_PLUGINS. ILDJIT uses one optimization levels plugin at a time. It uses the first one it finds inside the directories specified by ILDJIT_OPTIMIZATION_LEVELS_PLUGINS; if it did not find any one, it uses the default one installed inside the system (the one described in Sect. 4.2.1)

Hence, consider for example the following case:

```
$export ILDJIT_OPTIMIZATION_LEVELS_PLUGINS=/a;/b
```

Assuming that ILDJIT has been installed inside the default directory, which is /usr/local, ILDJIT uses the first plugin it is able to find at boost time in the following sorted directories: /a, /a and, if it was not able to find any one, /usr/local/lib/iljit/optimization_levels.

References

1. Appel, A.W.: Modern compiler implementation in Java. Cambridge University Press, Cambridge (2002)
2. Aho, A.V., Sethi, R., Ullman, J.D.: Compilers Principles, Techniques and Tools. Prentice Hall, NJ (2003)

3. Campanoni, S., Agosta, G., Crespi-Reghizzi, S., Di Biagio, A. A highly flexible, parallel virtual machine: design and experience of ILDJIT. Software: Practice and Experience. pp. 177–207 (2010)
4. Campanoni, S., Sykora, M., Agosta, G., Crespi-Reghizzi, S. Dynamic look ahead compilation: a technique to hide JIT compilation latencies in multicore environment. International conference on compiler construction. pp. 220–235 (2009)

Chapter 5
Intermediate Representation (IR)

Abstract Code optimizations play an important role inside a compiler. ILDJIT provides an intermediate representation (IR) to use for optimizing the code. After a brief description of this language, both its instructions set and its data types are introduced. Finally, an API provided by ILDJIT to use for transforming the code is described.

Keywords Compiler intermediate representation · Instructions set · Data types · Code transformations API

As other compilers, ILDJIT [1] has its own intermediate representation called IR, which breaks the compilation process into two main tasks: the translation from the input language (e.g. CIL) to the IR language and the successive generation of the machine code of the target platform starting from that intermediate representation. The produced IR code can be observed and manipulated by both several modules and external plugins of ILDJIT. For example, optimization levels plugins (see Chap. 4) can navigate the IR code in order to decide which set of optimizations to apply to it. Moreover, code optimization algorithms need to both read and modify the IR code to perform their code transformations. Finally, garbage collectors, which are components that manage the memory allocated at runtime, can need to both read and modify IR code in order to implement their memory collection algorithms (e.g. generational garbage collectors need to modify the code to maintain information about links across objects).

The IR language is designed to preserve the same amount of information of the currently supported input language, which is CIL. It is a platform independent language composed by an unbounded number of variables. IR instructions are similar to a RISC like ISA with both some high level operations, such as square root of values, and some classic operations of object oriented languages, such as throw exceptions or check if an address is zero or not.

After providing a high level description of the IR language, types of IR instructions that can appear inside methods are described. This chapter continues by describing

S. Campanoni, *Guide to ILDJIT*, SpringerBriefs in Computer Science, 41
DOI: 10.1007/978-1-4471-2194-7_5, © Simone Campanoni 2011

Fig. 5.1 Sequence of IR
instructions kept in memory
by ILDJIT and their relative
positions

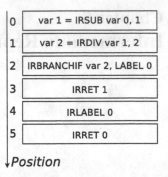

the data types available inside the IR language. Finally, a description of the interface
called IR API, which can be used to both observe and manipulate IR code, is provided.

5.1 The Language

A program described using the IR language is composed by methods. Each of them is
described by a set of instructions stored sequentially inside the method they belong to.
Figure 5.1 shows how a method is logically described by the IR language. Notice that
in this representation, the instruction at position i does not have to be the one executed
immediately after the instruction stored at position $i - 1$. The main advantage of
this representation is that it can be easily compressed in memory and sequential
iterations across instructions can be implemented efficiently. The IR API can be
used by external plugins, such as code tools described in Chap. 6, to access these IR
methods.

The IR language is composed by both data types and instructions. Data values,
which are always typed, can be constants or stored inside variables. Every instruction
can have from zero up to three parameters; also, instructions can have a result if
they produce some value. Moreover, they can have an unlimited number of *call
parameters*, which are considered only inside call instructions. Some instruction can
throw an exception at runtime for its execution corner cases, such as a value overflow.

Hence, every IR instruction type is described providing information about the
semantic of the instruction, its parameters and its call parameters. For example,
instructions of type `IRADDOVF` perform an addition operation on its first two parameters and it stores the produced value inside its result. Moreover, this instruction
has no call parameters and it throws an exception in case of overflow.

An example of this instruction type is the following:

```
var x = IRADDOVF var y, var z
```

which performs the sequence of operations described by the following pseudo code:

```
var x = var y + var z
if (overflow) throw exception;
```

Another example of IR instruction type is `IRADD` which is the same as `IRADDOVF`, but it cannot throw exceptions at runtime. For example, consider the following instruction:

```
var x = IRADDOVF var y, var z
```

The above instruction performs the following operation:

```
var x = var y + var z
```

5.2 Instructions

IR instructions are grouped in non overlapped sets based on their semantic. Each of these groups is following described by providing both a description of their instructions and some example of code that contains them.

5.2.1 Mathematic Operations

The first set is composed by mathematic operations like addition (i.e., `IRADD`, `IRADDOVF`), subtraction (i.e., `IRSUB`, `IRSUBOVF`), multiplication (i.e., `IRMUL`, `IRMULOVF`) division (i.e., `IRDIV`), computation of the reminder of a division operation (i.e., `IRREM`) and negation of a value (i.e., `IRNEG`). Other than these simple operations, the mathematic set is composed by more complex ones: computation of a square root of a value (i.e., `IRSQRT`), raise a value to the power of another one (i.e., `IRPOW`), the hyperbolic cosine of a value (i.e., `IRCOSH`), the sine of a value (i.e., `IRSIN`), the cosine of a value (i.e., `IRCOS`), the arc cosine of a value (i.e., `IRACOS`) and the computation of the largest integral value that is not greater than a given value (i.e., `IRFLOOR`).

For example, consider the following C# code:

```
int source_function(int p1, int p2){
  a = p1 + p2;
  d = a * 4;
  return d ;
}
```

An equivalent representation of the above method in the IR language is the following:

```
var 2 [IRINT32] = IRADD var 0, var 1
var 3 [IRINT32] = IRMUL var 2, 4
IRRET var 3
```

5.2.2 Compare Operations

Instructions that belong to the second set perform comparison operations. Two values can be compared to check if the first one is less than the second one (i.e., IRLT); a similar comparison can be performed to check if the first value is greater than the second one (i.e., IRGT). Moreover, the equal comparison can be performed (i.e., IREQ). Finally, three more comparisons can be performed to check whether a value is not a number (i.e., IRISNAN), whether it is infinite (i.e., IRISINF) or whether an address is zero (i.e., IRCHECKNULL).

For example, consider the following C# code:

```
int source_function2 (int p1, int p2){
  return p1 > p2;
}
```

An equivalent representation of the above method in the IR language is the following:

```
var 2 [IRINT32] = IRGT var 0, var 1
IRRET var 2
```

5.2.3 Bitwise Operations

The third set is composed by bitwise operations like and (i.e., IRAND), or (i.e., IROR), xor (i.e., IRXOR), not (i.e., IRNOT), a left shifting of bits (i.e., IRSHL) and the right one (i.e., IRSHR).

For example, consider the following C# code:

```
int source_function2 (int p1, int p2){
  return p1 » p2;
}
```

An equivalent representation of the above method in the IR language is the following:

```
var 2 [IRINT32] = IRSHR var 0, var 1
IRRET var 2
```

5.2.4 Jump Instructions

Instructions that can jump to other ones that are not stored next to the them belong to the forth set. Different types of jumps can be performed from the usual ones, such as unconditional jump (i.e., IRBRANCH) and conditional jumps (i.e., IRBRANCHIF and IRBRANCHIFNOT), to the more complex jumps where the execution jumps

or not depending on whether the last instruction executed belongs to a given code
region or not (i.e., IRBRANCHIFPCNOTINRANGE). This type of jump can be used
to implement the execution model related to exceptions, which is typical to object
oriented languages such as Java or C#. For example, consider the following C# code:

```
void my_method (int a){
  a = a + 1;
  try{
    a = a + 2;
  } catch (Exception e){
    return 1};
  }
  return 0};
}
```

A possible equivalent representation of the above method by using the IR language
is the following:

```
IRINT32 my_method (var 0 [IRINT32]){
  IRUSESCATCHER
  var 0 =IRADDOVF var 0, 1
  IRLABEL 0
  var 0 = IRADDOVF var 0, 2
  IRLABEL 1
  IRRET var 0
  IRSTARTCATCHER
  IRBRANCHIFPCNOTINRANGE LABEL 0, LABEL 1, LABEL 2
  IRRET 1
  IRLABEL 2
  IRRETHROWUNHANDLED
  IREXITNODE
}
```

The execution of the above IR method is the following: it increases the first parameter of the method by one, then it tries to increase the result of the first instruction
by 2; if an overflow occurs, then the execution jumps to the IRSTARTCATCHER
instruction, which is later described. Inside the catcher of the exception, the position
inside the code where the exception has been thrown is checked: if it was not inside
the try block specified in C# (i.e., between IRLABEL 0 and IRLABEL 1), then
the execution jumps to the label IRLABEL 2 and it re-throws the exception to the
caller of the current method; otherwise, if the exception has been thrown from the
try block, the method returns the value one to its callee. Finally, if no exception has
been thrown, the method returns the value zero to its callee. The possible successors
of each instruction are described by the *Control Flow Graph* (*CFG*) [2], which is
a graph where nodes are basic blocks. A basic block is an instructions sequence
where each instruction, which is not the last one, has only one possible successor:
the one stored next to it; moreover, each instruction that is not the first one has only

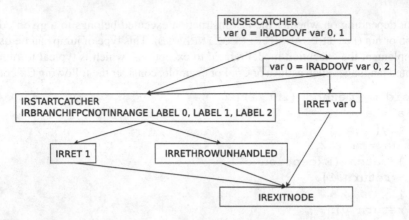

Fig. 5.2 Example of a Control Flow Graph (CFG) by using IR code

one possible predecessor: the one stored just before it. Finally, edges of the CFG represent the possible successors of the last instruction of basic blocks. The CFG of the above example is shown in Fig. 5.2.

Other than the types of jump already described above, jumps across methods are possible, such as calls and returns to the caller of the method currently in execution (i.e., IRRET).

Different types of direct calls (i.e., the address of the called method is known at compile time) are possible: direct calls to IR methods (i.e., IRCALL), direct calls to the native methods that belong to CIL libraries (i.e., IRLIBRARYCALL), where the body of the called methods are not described in IR because they are built inside the runtime system, and finally direct calls to methods not available in IR that do not belong to CIL libraries (i.e., IRNATIVECALL).

Indirect calls (i.e., the address of the called method is not known at compile time) are also possible: indirect calls that can jump to any method with a signature compatible with the one provided inside the instruction (i.e., IRICALL) and indirect calls where the called method depends on the dynamic type of an object (i.e., IRVCALL).

Finally, an instruction IREXIT concludes the execution of the entire program.

5.2.5 Memory Allocation Operations

In order to allocate memory at runtime, the IR language includes operations to allocate both single objects (i.e., IRNEWOBJ) and single arrays (i.e., IRNEWARR). Moreover, memory without a predefined semantic attached to it (like in the previous cases) can be allocated inside either the memory heap (i.e., IRALLOC and IRALLOCALIGN) or inside the memory stack (i.e., IRALLOCA). In the second case, the allocation frame of the method in execution increases by the amount of bytes specified as first parameter of the instruction. Finally, instruction types to free the memory previously allocated are provided: IRFREEOBJ frees a memory previously allocated either by IRNEWOBJ or by IRNEWARR. Moreover, IRFREE frees a memory previously allocated by an instruction IRALLOC. For example, the following IR method is valid:

```
IRVOID my_method2 (var 0 [IRINT32]) {
  var 1 [IROBJECT] = IRNEWOBJ CLASS MyClass
  var 2 [IRNINT] = IRALLOC 58
  IRFREEOBJ var 1
  IRFREE var 2
  IRRET
  IREXITNODE
}
```

The above method allocates an instance of the class MyClass, it allocates 58 bytes inside the memory heap, it frees these allocated memories and finally it returns to its callee.

5.2.6 Memory Access Operations

Memory access operations are provided inside the IR language. Operations that access previously allocated arrays are the following ones: IRLOADELEM, which loads a given element of an array, and IRSTOREELEM, which stores a value inside a given element of an array. Loads and stores to any type of memory are possible by using the instructions IRLOADREL and IRSTOREREL respectively. For example, the following IR method stores a value loaded from an object at offset ten to the fifth element of an array given as input.

```
IRVOID my_method3 (var 0 [IROBJECT],var 1 [IROBJECT]) {
  var 2 [IRINT32] = IRLOADREL var 0, 10, IRINT32
  IRSTOREELEM var 1, 4, var 2
  IRRET
  IREXITNODE
}
```

Notice that the type of the variable that points to an array is IROBJECT ; hence, arrays are objects inside the IR language.

5.2.7 Handling Exceptions

Instructions related to runtime exceptions are here described. An exception can be thrown in two different ways: if an exception object is catchable inside the method where it has been thrown, then an instruction IRTHROW is used. Otherwise, if an exception cannot be cached by the current method, and therefore it is thrown to the callee of the method in execution, an instruction IRRETHROWUNHANDLED is used. The exception thrown can be stored inside a variable by using an instruction IRTHROWNEXCEPTIONOBJECT. Moreover, the instruction IRSTARTCATCHER defines the point in the code where exceptions thrown by either the current method or methods called from it are handled. Methods that do not have this instruction throw exceptions to their callee directly; if the entry point of the program does not handle a thrown exception, the execution of the program aborts with an error message, which describes the call stack from the code where the exception has been created and thrown. On the other hand, methods able to handle exceptions have to insert an instruction IRUSESCATCHER at the begin of the method.

Every method can have one IRSTARTCATCHER instruction at most. The instruction IRBRANCHIFPCNOTINRANGE is used to handle more catch blocks in a single method, which are possible in object oriented languages like Java or C#.

A special way to handle exceptions, called filters, is provided inside the IR language. Filters are embedded subroutines within functions that are used to filter exceptions in catch blocks. Instructions IRSTARTFILTER and IRENDFILTER define their starts and their ends respectively. Finally, instructions IRCALLFILTER jump to a specific filter.

The following example throws an exception if the first parameter (i.e., var 0) is different than 5. The exception is handled by the method only if its second parameter (i.e., var 1) is different than 0.

```
IRVOID my_method4 (var 0 [IRINT32], var 1 [IRINT32]) {
   IRUSESCATCHER
   var 2 = IREQ var 0, 5
   IRBRANCHIF var 2, IRLABEL 0
   var 3 = IRNEWOBJ CLASS MyException
   IRTHROW var 3
   IRLABEL 0
   IRRET
   IRSTARTCATCHER
   IRBRANCHIF var 1, IRLABEL 1
   IRRETHROWUNHANDLED
   IRLABEL 1
   IRRET
   IREXITNODE
}
```

The CFG of the above example is shown in Fig. 5.3.

5.2.8 Miscellaneous Instructions

Instructions that do not belong to any of the previous classifications belong to this group. In this set there is the copy operation (i.e., IRCP), which copies a value from a variable to another one. Also, there are conversion operations, which convert

Fig. 5.3 Example of a
Control Flow Graph (CFG)
by using IR code

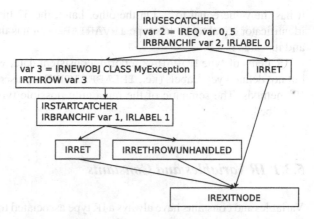

values to a given type (i.e., IRCONV and IRCONVOVF). Labels belong to this set also (i.e., IRLABEL). Moreover, it is possible to get the address of a variable (i.e., IRGETADDRESS). Special blocks called finally can be used inside IR code. A finally block is a piece of code that will be executed no matter what happen inside a method. Instructions IRSTARTFINALLY and IRENDFINALLY define the start and end of them respectively. Moreover, the instruction IRCALLFINALLY jumps to a finally block. Nop instructions (i.e., instructions that do not perform any kind of operation at runtime) can be used as well (i.e., IRNOP). Instructions ϕ, which are needed for a special form of the code called *Static Single Assignment* (*SSA*), are available inside the IR language (i.e., IRPHI). The unique exit point of every method is always a IREXITNODE instruction. Hence, every instruction that can conclude the execution of a method (e.g., IRRET) has IREXITNODE as single successor.

5.3 Data Types

IR elements of the IR language that are not instructions, which are called IR items and they are described by using the ILDJIT data structure ir_item_t defined inside the file ir_method.h, have a type, an internal type and a value. Moreover, these items can have an high level description of them, whose semantic depends on both their type and their internal type.

The item type describes its type, which can be a variable (i.e., IRVARIABLE), a constant (i.e., IRCONSTANT), a symbol (i.e., IRSYMBOL), an IR type descriptor (i.e., IRTYPE), a label (i.e., IRLABELITEM) or it can be undefined (i.e., NOPARAM).

The internal type of an item distinguishes the sub-cases of that relative item type. For example, the internal type of the type IRCONSTANT is the actual IR type of the constant (e.g. IRINT32).

The value of an item represents the actual value of that item whose semantic depends on both the type and the internal type of the item. For example, the 32 bit integer constant 5 has type IRCONSTANT, it has the internal type IRINT32 and it has the value equal to 5. On the other hand, the 32 bit integer variable with the identificator equal to 10 has type IRVARIABLE, it has the internal type IRINT32 and its value is 10.

IR items of type NOPARAM report inconsistent data, which has been initialized, but not defined yet. Labels (i.e., IRLABELITEM) are used to define positions inside IR methods. The semantic of the remaining possible types of items are following described.

5.3.1 IR Variables and Constants

Variables and constants have always a IR type associated to them, which is defined by the internal type of their correspondent item; they can have an high level description of their type that depends on the input language used by ILDJIT (e.g. CIL). For example, an instance of a class MyClass has the IR type, which is equal to the item internal type, IROBJECT and it has an high level description of MyClass, which reports information about it, such as number, names and offsets of fields that compose that class.

The header ir_language.h, which is available in the system after having installed ILDJIT, describes the available IR types, which include integer, floating point and pointers types. Integer and floating point types include both the ones with a specific number of bits from 8 to 64 (e.g. IRINT32, IRFLOAT32) and those where the number of bits depends on the size of the word of the processor of the underlying platform (e.g. 64 for 64 bit processors), which are IRNINT for signed integer values, IRNUINT for unsigned ones and IRNFLOAT for floating point values.

Memory addresses of memory locations with a given semantic can be stored inside pointer types following described. In case of no information about the memory location pointed by a variable or constant is available, the type IRNUINT, which always has the same number of bits of a memory address, is used. Even if it would be possible to declare every variable or constant representing a memory address as IRNUINT, other IR types are available in the language to describe additional constraints of these addresses. Notice that declaring variables or constants with a type that best describe them is important to help code optimization algorithms to exploit this information in order to produce better code.

For addresses of the first byte of an object, the type IROBJECT is used if that object is not an instance of the class String; for instances of the class String, the type IRSTRING is used. For addresses of any field of an object, the type IRMPOINTER is used. Moreover, for addresses of methods, the type IRFPOINTER is used. Finally, for variables or constants that store addresses of descriptors of classes, methods or signatures, the types IRCLASSID, IRMETHODID and IRSIGNATURE are used respectively.

Other than integer, floating point and pointer values, complex structure data types can be used in IR programs; variables or constants that store these structures have the IR type IRVALUETYPE.

5.3.2 IR Symbols

Symbols can be used inside the IR language to produce position independent code. For example, a memory address, whose value can change across different program executions, can be described by a logical symbol inside the language, which is kept constant across different runs. Symbols are translated to their correspondent values during the generation of the machine code. This translation process is called *symbol resolution* and it is performed by calling the following functions, which belong to the IR API:

```
ir_value_t IRMETHOD_resolveSymbol(
  ir_symbol_t *symbol);
void IRMETHOD_ resolveSymbolFromIRItem(
  r_ item_ t *item,
  ir_ item_t *resolvedSymbol);
```

New symbols can be defined by using the IR API and, in order to do that, the module that defines a new symbol has to register itself as the one in charge to perform the resolution of every instance of that symbol. The registration of a new symbol is performed by providing a set of function pointers of methods usually provided by the module that is defining that symbol. These methods are in charge to resolve, serialize to a file, deserialize from a file and dump to a file instances of that symbol. The function to use, which belongs to the IR API, to create a new symbol is the following one:

```
void IRMETHOD_registerSymbolDeserializer(
  JITUINT32 tag,
  ir_value_ t (*resolve)(
    ir_symbol_t *symbol,
  void (*serialize)(
    ir_symbol_t * symbol),
    FILE *fileToWrite),
  void (*dump)(
    ir_symbol_t *symbol,
    FILE *fileToWrite),
  ir_symbol_t * (*deserialize)(
    FILE * fileToRead));
```

The first parameter, tag, is the identificator of the new symbol that is going to be registered.

The following example registers a new symbol 15, which can correspond to either the address of a global variable called my_global_var or the address of another one called my_global_var2.

```
JITUINT32 my_global_var;
JITUINT32 my_global_var2;
...
```

```
IRMETHOD_registerSymbolDeserializer(
  15,
  my_symbol_resolve,
  my_symbol_serialize,
  my_symbol_dump,
  my_symbol_deserialize);
```

The bodies of the above functions given as parameters are following described.

The following serialize function transforms the value that can change across different program executions to a fixed pre-defined value. In our case, values 1 and 2 are assigned to the global variables my_global_var and my_global_var2 respectively. This function is called every time the IR code is going to be stored inside the code cache of ILDJIT.

```
void my_symbol_ serialize(
  ir_symbol_t * symbol,
  FILE *fileToWrite) {
  if (symbol->data == &my_global_var)
    fprintf(fileToWrite, "1");
  } else {
    fprintf(fileToWrite, "2");
  }
}
```

The following resolve function is called during the generation of the target machine code in order to transform a symbol to its actual value needed to run the program effectively. In order to do that, values 1 and 2 have to be translated to the addresses of their correspondent variables.

```
ir_value_t my_symbol_resolve (
  ir_symbol_t *symbol) {
  if (symbol->data == 1) {
    return &my_global_var ;
  }
  return &my_global_var2;
}
```

The following deserialize function is called as soon as the IR code is loaded from the code cache. In our case no translation is needed.

```
ir_symbol_t * static_object_deserialize(
  FILE *fileToRead) {
  JITUINT32 symbolID;
  if (fscanf(fileToRead, "%u", &symbolID) == 0) {
        abort();
  }
  ir_symbol_t *symbol = IRMETHOD_loadSymbol(
    symbolID);
```

```
return IRMETHOD_createSymbol(
  STATIC_OBJECT_SYMBOL,
  (void *) IRMETHOD_resolveSymbol(symbol).v);
}
```

Finally, the following dump function is called every time the IR code needs to be dumped in some human readable form. This function is called every time ILDJIT needs to have a human readable representation of symbols (e.g. to plot CFGs).

```
void static_object_dump (
  ir_symbol_t *symbol,
  FILE *fileToWrite){
  if (symbol->data == my_global_var) {
    fprintf(fileToWrite, "my_global_var");
  } else {
    fprintf(fileToWrite, "my_global_var2");
  }
}
```

5.3.3 IR Type Descriptors

An IR item can be a descriptor of an IR type, such as IRINT32. In this case, the item type to use is IRTYPE and the value of the item is the IR type that we want to use.

For example, consider the conversion instruction IRCONV; the first parameter is the variable, or constant, that we want to convert. The second parameter is the type that we want to convert the value into, which is described by an item of type IRTYPE.

For example, an IR instruction that converts a variable into a floating point value has the second parameter, which is an item, with both type and internal type equal to IRTYPE. Moreover, the value of this item is equal to IRFLOAT32.

As previously, an item of this type can have an high level description of the type that represents.

5.4 IR API

In order to either read or modify IR code, the interface IR API defined inside the file ir_method.h is provided by ILDJIT. Functions of this interface provide both simple information about IR code, like how many parameters has a given instruction, and complex information, such as how many loops are defined inside a method or what are the possible methods callable from a given indirect call.

Some information requested by some functions, which belongs to the IR API, can become invalid due to a successive modification of the IR code. For example, information about instructions that belong to a given loop can become invalid suddenly if we move some of those instructions outside that loop. One of the code transformations that modify the IR code in this way is the *loop invariant code motion* [2].

Since ILDJIT can be used as a dynamic compiler as well, the option of recomputing this corrupted information every time there is a possibility that some change to the code can make it invalid is too expensive. Consider that, since ILDJIT is an automatic tool, it has to make conservative assumptions to the problem of understanding which changes to the code invalid a given information. Instead, the framework relies to the user of the IR API that has to ensure that the information read by a given function, which is described inside the documentation of the IR API, is valid at the time that function is called. In case this information is not valid (because the user knows that he, or she, did some change to the code, which made it invalid), the user can asks to ILDJIT to recompute that specific information paying the correspondent overhead.

For example, consider the following function, which is part of the IR API:

```
XanList * IRMETHOD_getLoopInstructions(
  ir_method_t* method,
  t_loop *loop);
```

In this case, the documentation of this function declares that the information about loops inside the method specified as first parameter have to be valid whenever the returned list is used. Assuming that the user is writing a plugin as following:

```
XanList *l;
l = IRMETHOD_getLoopInstructions(
  method,
  code_loop);
move_loop_invariants(l);
l2 = IRMETHOD_getLoopInstructions(
  method,
  code_loop);
use_list_of_loop_instructions(l2);
```

The code starts getting the list of instructions l that compose the loop `code_loop`; it moves some instructions outside the loop, it gets the list of instructions l2 of the same loop and finally it uses the new list l2. The list l at the first invocation of the function `IRMETHOD_getLoopInstructions` is valid. After moving instructions outside the loop, the list l is not valid anymore. Moreover, when the user calls `IRMETHOD_getLoopInstructions` for the second time, the returned list l2 is not valid as well. The only possible solution that can be applied by ILDJIT to resolve this problem is to recompute the loop information inside the second call of `IRMETHOD_getLoopInstructions`, which slows down the execution of the plugin written by the user drastically. Another solution is that the user, who knows the semantic of his, or her, piece of code, updates the returned list l properly avoiding

the second call. A correct implementation of the code previously described is the
following:

```
XanList *l;
l = IRMETHOD_getLoopInstructions (
  method,
  code_loop);
move_loop_invariants_and_update_list(l);
use_list_of_loop_instructions(l);
```

In this case, when the user moves instructions outside the loop, it updates the
list by removing them from l as well. Hence, at the time that list is used inside
use_list_of_loop_instructions, the list l is still valid. Notice that any
automatic solution implemented inside ILDJIT can lead to useless re-computations
of these information, which can slow down significantly the execution of the module
that is using the IR API.

IR instructions can be both read and iterated by following different relations over
them, which are described in the next sections.

5.4.1 Iterating Across IR Code

There are two different ways of iterating across IR code by using the IR API, which
are used for different purposes: by following the way instructions, or basic blocks,
are stored inside ILDJIT or by following the successor (or the predecessor) relation
across them. Each type of iteration can be performed at two different levels: at
instruction level or at basic block level.

5.4.1.1 Instructions Level

As previously discussed, ILDJIT stores instructions of a method sequentially. Each
instruction has its position, which is relative to the begin of this sequence. Hence,
the first instruction of the method is stored at position zero, the second one is stored
at position one and so on. Functions available inside the IR API to iterate through
this sequence are the following ones:

```
t_ir_instruction * IRMETHOD_getFirstInstruction (
  ir_method_t *method);
t_ir_instruction * IRMETHOD_getLastInstruction (
  ir_method_t *method);
t_ir_instruction * IRMETHOD_getNextInstruction (
  ir_method_t *method,
  t_ir_instruction *inst);
t_ir_instruction * IRMETHOD_getPrevInstruction (
```

Fig. 5.4 Next and prev
relations between IR
instructions

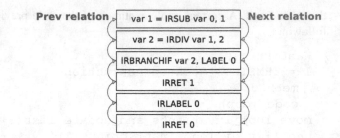

```
    ir_method_t *method,
    t_ir_instruction *inst);
  t_ir_instruction * IRMETHOD_getInstructionAtPosition(
    ir_method_t *method,
    JITUINT32 position);
JITUINT32 IRMETHOD_getInstructionsNumber(
    ir_method_t *method);
```

The above functions use the relation *next* and *prev*, which iterate through the
instructions stored sequentially. Figure 5.4 shows these relations applied to an
example of IR code.

For example, the following code iterates across every instruction of a method
starting from its entry point by using the next relation:

```
t_ir_instruction *i;
t_ir_instruction *last;
last = IRMETHOD_getLastInstruction(method);
i = IRMETHOD_getFirstInstruction(method);
do {
  i = IRMETHOD_getNextInstruction(method, i);
} while (i != last);
```

The next example iterates across instructions as the previous example did, but it
does that by using the positions of the instructions explicitly:

```
JITUINT32 pos;
JITUINT32 maxPos;
maxPos = IRMETHOD_getInstructionsNumber(method);
for (pos=0; pos < maxPos; pos++) {
  t_ir_instruction *i;
  i = IRMETHOD_getInstructionAtPosition(method, pos);
}
```

Instructions can be iterated by using either the successor or predecessor relation.
These relations consider the possible instructions that can be executed either after or
before a given one. Hence, by using these relations, we are able to traverse the CFG.

Fig. 5.5 Successor and
predecessor relations
between IR instructions

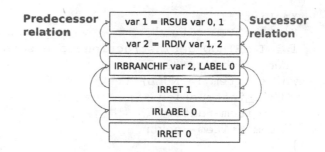

Figure 5.5 shows the successor and predecessor relations applied to an example of
IR code.

Functions to get successors of a given instruction are the following:

```
t_ir_instruction * IRMETHOD_getSuccessorInstruction(
    ir_method_t *method,
    t_ir_instruction *inst,
    t_ir_instruction *prevSuccessor);
XanList * IRMETHOD_getInstructionSuccessors(
    ir_method_t *method,
    t_ir_instruction *inst);
JITUINT32 IRMETHOD_getSuccessorsNumber(
    ir_method_t *method,
    t_ir_instruction *inst);
```

The function `IRMETHOD_getSuccessorInstruction` returns one
successor at a time. On the other hand, the function `IRMETHOD_getInstruction`
`Successors` returns the full list of possible successors altogether.

For example, the following code iterates over every possible successor of an
instruction j given as input:

```
void my_code (
    ir_method_t *method,
    t_ir_instruction *j){
    t_ir_instruction *i;
    i = IRMETHOD_getSuccessorInstruction(method, j, NULL);
    while (i != NULL) {
        i = IRMETHOD_getSuccessorInstruction(method, j, i);
    }
}
```

The following example iterates over successors of an instruction by fetching them
altogether:

```
void my_code2 (
    ir_method_t *method,
    t_ir_instruction *j){
```

```
XanList *l;
XanListItem *item;
l = IRMETHOD_getInstructionSuccessors(method, j);
item = l->first(l);
while (item != NULL) {
  t_ir_instruction *i;
  i = item->data;
  item = item->next;
}
l->destroyList(l);
}
```

Notice that in this example, we have to destroy the returned list that declare possible successors of an instruction. In case of the successor relation is often used without changing the code, we can speedup the execution of the module we are implementing by caching successors of instructions like in the following example:

```
JITUINT32 count;
JITUINT32 num;
XanList **successors;
XanListItem *item;

/* Fetch the number of instructions */
num = IRMETHOD_getInstructionsNumber(
  method);

/* Cache the successors */
successors = malloc(sizeof(XanList *) * num);
for (count = 0; count < num; count++) {
  t_ir_instruction *inst;
  inst = IRMETHOD_getInstructionAtPosition(
    method,
    count);
  successors[count] = IRMETHOD_getInstructionSuccessors(
    method,
    inst);
}

/* Iterates over successors of the first instruction */
j = IRMETHOD_getFirstInstruction(
    method);
count = JITUINT32 IRMETHOD_getInstructionPosition(
    j);
successors[count]->first(successors[count]);
while (item != NULL) {
    t_ir_instruction *s;
```

```
    s = item->data;
    item = item->next;
}

/* Free the memory */
for (count = 0; count < num; count++) {
  successors[count]->destroyList(successors[count]);
}
free(successors);
```

A code that often uses the successor relation executes faster by caching this relation, as described by the previous example, rather than using the function IRMETHOD_getSuccessorInstruction for every access.

A symmetric set of functions are provided inside the IR API to use the predecessor relation. Functions to use to traverse instructions by using this relation are the following:

```
t_ir_instruction * IRMETHOD_getPredecessorInstruction(
  ir_method_t *method,
  t_ir_instruction *inst,
  t_ir_instruction *prevPredecessor);
XanList * IRMETHOD_getInstructionPredecessors(
  ir_method_t *method,
  t_ir_instruction *inst);
JITUINT32 IRMETHOD_getPredecessorsNumber(
  ir_method_t *method,
  t_ir_instruction *inst);
```

5.4.1.2 Basic Blocks Level

IR code can be read by using information about basic blocks. To remind, a basic block is an instructions sequence where each one, which is not the last one, has one possible successor: the one stored next to it. Moreover, each instruction of a basic block that is not the first one has only one possible predecessor: the one stored just before it.

As for instructions, we have next and prev relations across basic blocks. The functions available inside the IR API to use for these relations are the following:

```
BasicBlock * IRMETHOD_getFirstBasicBlock(
  ir_method_t *method);
BasicBlock * IRMETHOD_getLastBasicBlock(
  ir_method_t *method);
BasicBlock * IRMETHOD_getNextBasicBlock(
  ir_method_t *method,
  BasicBlock *bb);
```

Fig. 5.6 Next and prev
relations between basic
blocks of IR code

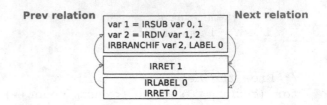

```
BasicBlock * IRMETHOD_getPrevBasicBlock(
  ir_method_t *method,
  BasicBlock *bb);
BasicBlock * IRMETHOD_getBasicBlockAtPosition(
  ir_method_t *method,
  JITUINT32 position);
JITUINT32 IRMETHOD_getNumberOfMethodBasicBlocks(
  ir_method_t *method);
```

Figure 5.6 shows the next and prev relations across basic blocks of the code shown in Fig. 5.4.

For example, the following code iterates across basic blocks of a method as they are stored in memory:

```
BasicBlock *b;
b = IRMETHOD_getFirstBasicBlock(method);
while (b != NULL) {
  b = IRMETHOD_getNextBasicBlock(
    method,
    b);
}
```

As for instructions, successors and predecessors of basic blocks can be accessed either one at a time or altogether. The functions available inside the IR API to access them are the following ones:

```
BasicBlock * IRMETHOD_getSuccessorBasicBlock(
  ir_method_t *method,
  BasicBlock *bb,
  BasicBlock *prevSuccessor);
XanList * IRMETHOD_getBasicBlockSuccessors(
  ir_method_t *method,
  BasicBlock *bb);
JITUINT32 IRMETHOD_getBasicBlockSuccessorsNumber(
  ir_method_t *method,
  BasicBlock *bb);
BasicBlock * IRMETHOD_getPredecessorBasicBlock(
  ir_method_t *method,
  BasicBlock *bb,
```

Fig. 5.7 Successor and predecessor relations between IR basic blocks

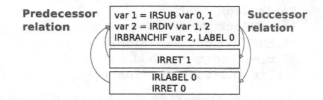

Figure 5.7 shows the successor and predecessor relations between basic blocks in the same code shown in Fig. 5.5.

For example, the following code iterates over every possible successor of a basic block one at a time:

```
BasicBlock *prevPredecessor);
XanList * IRMETHOD_getBasicBlockPredecessors (
  ir_method_t *method,
  BasicBlock *bb);
JITUINT32 IRMETHOD_getBasicBlockPredecessorsNumber (
  ir_method_t *method,
  BasicBlock *bb);
```

Figure 5.7 shows the successor and predecessor relations between basic blocks in the same code shown in Fig. 5.5.

For example, the following code iterates over every possible successor of a basic block one at a time:

```
void my_code3 (
  ir_method_t *method,
  BasicBlock *b){
BasicBlock *bSuc;
bSuc = IRMETHOD_getSuccessorBasicBlock (
  method,
  b,
  NULL);
while (bSuc != NULL){
  bSuc = IRMETHOD_getSuccessorBasicBlock (
    method,
    b,
    bSuc);
  }
}
```

Finally, there are functions available inside the IR API to change the working level from the instruction level to the basic block level and vice versa. These functions are following declared:

```
t_ir_instruction *
  IRMETHOD_getFirstInstructionWithinBasicBlock (
  ir_method_t *method,
  BasicBlock *bb);
XanList * IRMETHOD_getInstructionsOfBasicBlock (
  ir_method_t *method,
```

```
BasicBlock *bb);
BasicBlock *
    IRMETHOD_getTheBasicBlockIncludesInstruction(
    ir_method_t *method,
    t_ir_instruction *inst);
```

An example of usage of the above functions is the following, which iterates over instructions of a given basic block:

```
void my_code4 (
    ir_method_t *method,
    BasicBlock *b){
XanList *l;
XanListItem *item;
l = IRMETHOD_getInstructionsOfBasicBlock (
    method,
    b);
item = l->first(l);
while (item != NULL) {
    t_ir_instruction *i;
    i = item->data;
    item = item->next;
    }
}
```

References

1. Campanoni, S., Agosta, G., Crespi-Reghizzi, S., Di Biagio, A.: A highly flexible, parallel virtual machine: design and experience of ILDJIT. Softw. Pract. Exp. **40**(2), 177–207 (2010)
2. Aho, A.V., Sethi, R., Ullman, J.D.: Compilers Principles, Techniques and Tools. Prentice Hall, Upper Saddle River (2003)

Chapter 6
Analyzing and Transforming Programs

Abstract Code transformations are useful for different purposes, such as improving performance, reducing memory used at runtime, reducing power consumed by the program, and so on. Usually, code transformations rely on code analysis applied either at static time or at runtime (i.e., code profiling). This chapter describes how to implement both code analysis and code transformations inside ILDJIT by describing the interface between them and the framework. Finally, several examples are both provided and described.

Keywords Code optimizations · Code analysis · Code profiling

Understanding the execution of a program is essential to transform it for optimizing metrics like performance, memory used or power consumed. Two main approaches are often used to infer both the semantic of a program and the impact of its execution on a given architecture: code analysis and code profiling.

The first one, which is also called static code analysis, is an algorithm usually executed without the intervention of a human, which takes as input the code of the program and it produces as output the information for whom this tool was designed for. This kind of analysis is input-independent, which means that the information inferred is valid for every program execution. An example of this type of information is the total number of variables used by a given method. Another example is the minimum number of instructions executed by a given piece of code.

The second approach, code profiling, is a technique used to monitor the behavior of a program at runtime. This analysis is often performed by injecting additional code inside the program, which dynamically monitor some specific information. The input of a code profiler is both a program and its input to be used for the analysis; hence, the profiled information is input-dependent. The output can be either a statistical summary of the events observed (i.e., profile), such as the number of instructions executed overall, or a stream of recorded events (i.e., trace), which is usually later analyzed by another tool.

Armed with the information coming from either code analysis or code profiling, a program can be transformed in order to improve metrics like the overall execution

S. Campanoni, *Guide to ILDJIT*, SpringerBriefs in Computer Science,
DOI: 10.1007/978-1-4471-2194-7_6, © Simone Campanoni 2011

time. This operation of changing the program is called code transformation and it is usually performed by an automatic tool. This tool takes as input the output of previous analysis and it outputs the transformed program. An example of code transformation is the common sub-expression elimination already described in Chap. 4, where those expressions that are computed earlier in the code and that are still valid are removed being redundant.

Since the only limit on the number of different types of information that can be analyzed, as well as the possible code transformations, is the imagination, ILDJIT performs these tasks by completely relying on its customizations (i.e., external plugins). These external plugins are called *code tools*. The framework provides a shared solution for these tasks (i.e., code analysis, code profiling and code transformations) composed by both the already introduced IR API, which can be used by any code tool, and a set of functions that each plugin of this type has to implement. The last set of functions represent the *code tool API*, which is later described.

After describing how code tools can be installed inside the system to be used by ILDJIT, information about how code analysis and code profiling can be implemented inside this framework, by means of new code tools, is provided. Finally, this chapter describes how code transformations can be performed inside ILDJIT. Examples are provided for each of these aforementioned tasks.

6.1 Adding a New Code Tool

Code analysis, code profiling and code transformations are implemented by means of code tools, which are external plugins installed in the system that implement the correspondent task. Code tools can be installed only after that ILDJIT has been installed inside the system. Every code tool is an independent project with its own package composed by scripts, sources and documentations. ILDJIT provides a dummy package for code tools called `codetool-dummy`, which can be used as start point for new ones.

The interface between a code tool and ILDJIT is composed by the IR API defined inside the file `ir_method.h`. As described in Chap. 5, this API is composed by more than three hundred functions, which can be used to implement both code analysis and code transformation tasks. Examples of these functions are the following:

```
t_ir_instruction * IRMETHOD_getFirstInstruction (
    ir_method_t *method);
t_ir_instruction *
    IRMETHOD_newInstructionOfTypeBefore (
    ir_method_t *method,
    t_ir_instruction *prev,
    JITUINT16 instructionType);
```

An example of use of them is the following:

```
t_ir_instruction *i;
i = IRMETHOD_getFirstInstruction(method);
t_ir_instruction *
    IRMETHOD_newInstructionOfTypeBefore (
    method,
    i,
    IRRET);
```

The above piece of code introduces a return instruction as entry point of a method.

Both the compilation and installation of a new code tool, next described, follow the standard installation process of Linux like packages. In order to compile a new code tool, we need to go to the parent directory of the plugin. Hence, assuming that the code tool we want to install is the dummy one, we need to run the following commands:

```
$ cd codetool-dummy
$ ls
AUTHORS bootstrap ChangeLog configure.ac COPYING
INSTALL Makefile.am NEWS README src
```

The first step is to configure the code tool by running the following script:

```
$ ./configure
checking for a BSD-compatible install...
checking whether build environment is sane...
checking for a thread-safe mkdir -p...
...
```

Other than standard options, the script configure accepts three additional ones: --enable-debug, which enables assertions declared inside the plugin, it defines the macro DEBUG and it compiles the plugin by inserting symbols inside (to enable the execution inside debugger like gdb). Another option is --enable-profile, which compiles the program with symbols. Finally, the option --enable-printdebug enables the macro PDEBUG, defined inside the header file of the plugin, which should be used to print debugging messages.

Now that the code tool has been configured, we can compile it as following:

```
$ make
Making all in src
make[1]: Entering directory ...
make all-am
make[2]: Entering directory
...
```

It is time to install the new code tool inside the system by typing the following command:

```
$ make install
aking install in src
make[1]: Entering directory ...
make[2]: Entering directory
...
```

Assuming that both the compilation and installation succeed (hence, the implementation of the new code tool has no compilation error inside), we need to tell to ILDJIT where the new code tool has been installed. As in Sect. 2.4 and in Sect. 4.4.4, the solution is based on an environment variable, which is called ILDJIT_CODE_TOOL_PLUGINS. ILDJIT loads code tools as it is described in Sect. 2.4, where ILDJIT_CODE_TOOL_PLUGINS defines the list of directories used to install them. For example, if we installed code tools in two different directories, /a and /b, then we need to set the environment variable as following:

```
$ export ILDJIT_CODE_TOOL_PLUGINS=/a;/b
```

As described in Sect. 4.4.2, ILDJIT defines a set of identificators for both code analysis and code transformation tasks inside the file ir_optimizer.h. A code tool needs to declare which task, or tasks, is able to provide (like dead code elimination, variables liveness analysis, etc...). After the loading phase, ILDJIT keeps in memory only those code tools that implement tasks not yet provided by other plugins loaded earlier. This implies that the declaration order of directories provided by ILDJIT_CODE_TOOL_PLUGINS needs to reflect the wishes of the user. Remember that (see Sect. 4.4.2) ILDJIT loads code tools from directories specified by ILDJIT_CODE_TOOL_PLUGINS first, and then the ones available inside the directory where ILDJIT has been installed. Hence, if there are two code tools that provide the dead code elimination task installed in two different directories, say /a and /b, and we want to use the one installed in a, then we have to set ILDJIT_CODE_TOOL_PLUGINS as following:

```
$ export ILDJIT_CODE_TOOL_PLUGINS=/a;/b
```

6.2 Code Tool API

The code tool API defines the set of functions that code tools have to provide. This API is described inside the file ir_optimization_interface.h, which is available inside the system by installing the ILDJIT framework.

The functions that code tools have to implement are following described:

```
void        (*init)                     (
    ir_lib_t *irLib,
    ir_optimizer_t *optimizer,
    char *outputPrefix);
JITUINT64 (*get_job_kind)        (void);
JITUINT64 (*get_dependences)     (void);
```

```
JITUINT64 (*get_invalidations) (void);
void       (*do_job)            (
    ir_method_t *method);
char *     (*get_version)       (void);
char *     (*get_information)   (void);
char *     (*get_author) (void);
void       (*shutdown)      (JITFLOAT32 totalTime);
```

The function init is called when ILDJIT boosts, and in particular, it is called before any compilation task, such as code translation, is performed. This function is called once during the entire compilation, or execution, of a program. The user can add code to initialize his, or her, code tool here, such as opening files later used, initializing data structures, and so on.

The function shutdown is called just before ILDJIT shuts down the entire system; hence, it is called only once. The user can add code to shutdown his, or her, code tool here, such as closing files previously used, printing final results, and so on. The parameter of this function is the total time, in seconds, spent by ILDJIT during the current execution.

The function get_job_kind returns the set of tasks the code tool is able to perform. Every code tool has to provide one task at least, such as dead code elimination, variables liveness analysis, and so on.

The function get_invalidations returns the set of information that this code tool invalidates at most when it is applied to a method. For example, loop invariant code motion invalidates loops information; a copy propagation invalidates variables liveness analysis. Code tools that analyze the code and produce information about it do not invalidate nothing usually. Hence, this set will be empty for them. The most conservative solution implementable for this function is returning the value INVALIDATE_ALL, which includes every possible information.

The function get_dependences returns the set of information that the code tool needs to have before starting its execution. For example, loop invariant code motion needs loops information before applying its code transformation to the code. ILDJIT ensures that these information are always valid just before the correspondent code tool is invoked.

Finally, the function do_job is the heart of the code tool; it is the function that actually performs its tasks whose is designed for. This function is called only if the current code tool has been enabled, no matter what is the compilation scheme used (see Chap. 4). In case the code tool is enabled, how often this function is invoked depends on both the compilation scheme used and the optimization levels plugin used. Assuming that the optimization levels plugin calls a code tool once, then, for dynamic compilation schemes, the function do_job is called once per method. On the other hand, for static compilation schemes, the function do_job is called once during the entire compilation and execution of the program. For those, the method given as input to this function is the entry point of the program.

The rest of the chapter introduces examples of code tools for code analysis, code profiling and code transformation tasks.

6.3 Examples of Code Analysis

Consider the following code analysis: we want to write a code tool, which computes the total number of static instructions of those methods that are executed at runtime. One solution to write such code tool is following described.

First, we need to declare the functions that implement the code tool API. Inside our code tool file, say `my_code_tool.c`, we write the signatures of these functions.

```
JITUINT64 my_code_tool_get_ID_job (void);
char * my_code_tool_get_version (void);
void my_code_tool_do_job (
    ir_method_t * method);
char * my_code_tool_get_information (void);
char * my_code_tool_get_author (void);
JITUINT64 my_code_tool_get_dependences (void);
void my_code_tool_shutdown (
    JITFLOAT32 totalTime);
void my_code_tool_init (
    ir_lib_t *lib,
    ir_optimizer_t *optimizer,
    char *outputPrefix);
JITUINT64 my_code_tool_get_invalidations (void);
```

After having declared the above signatures, we can declare the global variables we need in our plugin. In our case, we only need the counter of the static instructions.

```
JITUINT64 totalStaticInstructionsNumber;
```

In order to enable ILDJIT to call the above functions when is needed, we have to attach them to the code tool API as following:

```
ir_optimization_interface_t plugin_interface = {
my_code_tool_get_ID_job ,
my_code_tool_get_dependences,
my_code_tool_init,
my_code_tool_shutdown,
my_code_tool_do_job,
my_code_tool_get_version,
my_code_tool_get_information,
my_code_tool_get_author,
my_code_tool_get_invalidations
};
```

The rest of the code tool is composed by the implementations of its functions previously declared. The code analysis we want to implement will be invoked inside the JIT compilation scheme. Moreover, we write the optimization levels plugin such as our code tool is called as last one. Hence, the IR code we analyze inside our tool is the actual code that will be translated to the target machine code.

The first function to implement is `my_code_tool_init`, which initializes the environment. In our case, we need to initialize the instructions counter as following:

```
void my_code_tool_init (
   ir_lib_t *lib,
   ir_optimizer_t *optimizer,
   char *outputPrefix){
   totalStaticInstructionsNumber = 0;
}
```

Since our code tool does not change the code, it does not invalidate anything. Hence,

```
JITUINT64 my_code_tool_get_invalidations (void);
   return 0;
}
```

Since we are not planning to provide the computed information to other plugins, our code tool can be declared as it provides the most generic task, which is called CUSTOM.

```
JITUINT64 my_code_tool_get_ID_job (void){
   return CUSTOM;
}
```

Our code tool does not use any information that needs to be computed. Hence, it has no dependences.

```
JITUINT64 my_code_tool_get_dependences (void){
   return 0;
}
```

Since we will know the total number of static instructions only at the end of the execution, we print this information inside the shutdown function.

```
void my_code_tool_shutdown (JITFLOAT32 totalTime){
   printf("My new code tool:\n
   total number of static instructions =%llu \n",
   totalStaticInstructionsNumber);
}
```

Finally, we provide the function that actually updates the counter of static instructions that compose the program.

```
void my_code_tool_do_job (
   ir_method_t * method){
   totalStaticInstructionsNumber +=
   IRMETHOD_getInstructionsNumber(method);
```

}

Other functions have to be provided, which includes information about both the name of the author and the version of the code tool. Their standard implementations are available inside the dummy code tool.

In order to use our plugin, we rely on the default optimization levels plugin, which invokes the code tool that provides the custom task inside the optimization level 3 as last one. Hence,

```
$ iljit -O3 hello_world_c.cil
Hello, world!
My new code tool:
    total number of static instructions = 150
$
```

Notice that our code tool computes correctly the total number of static instructions of executed methods because it is called (thanks to the JIT compilation scheme) just before generating the machine code of every method that the dynamic compiler is going to execute.

6.4 Examples of Code Profiling

Execution profiling by code injection adds additional code inside executed methods. For this reason, we usually need to ensure, by customizing the optimization levels accordingly (see Chap. 4), that the added code tool is called as last one by ILDJIT.

As example of code profiling, we want to compute the total number of instructions effectively executed at runtime. Our code tool is similar to the one described in Sect. 6.3, but in addition to that, we need to instrument the code.

The only function that we need to implement differently with respect to the previous code tool is the do_job one following described:

```
void my_code_tool_do_job (
   ir_method_t * method){
   t_ir_instruction *i;
   i = IRMETHOD_getFirstInstruction (
   method);
   while (i != NULL){
     if (!IRMETHOD_isALabelInstruction(
         i){
       IRMETHOD_newNativeCallInstructionBefore(
         method,
         i,
         "my_runtime_counter",
         my_runtime_counter,
         NULL,
         NULL);
```

```
}
i = IRMETHOD_getNextInstruction (
   method,
   i);
  }
}
void my_runtime_counter (void){
  totalStaticInstructionsNumber++;
}
```

Moreover, we need to change the final message printed by our plugin as following:

```
void my_code_tool_shutdown (JITFLOAT32 totalTime){
printf("My new code tool: \ n
   total number of dynamic instructions =%llu \ n",
   totalStaticInstructionsNumber);
}
```

Finally, in order to call our new code tool we use the default optimization levels plugin. Hence,

```
$ iljit -O3 hello_world_c.cil
Hello, world!
My new code tool:
     total number of dynamic instructions = 30
$
```

We can notice that the total number of instructions effectively executed is less than the total number of static instructions. The reason is that there is no loop inside our simple hello world program (otherwise the oppposite is likely to be true).

6.5 Examples of Code Optimizations

As example of a code optimization, we provide a code tool, which removes call instructions to methods that include a return instruction only.

The main difference of our code tool that we are going to implement, with respect to the previous two examples, is about the function do_job, which is following described.

```
void my_code_tool_do_job (
   ir_method_t * method){
   t_ir_instruction *i;

/* Allocate memory */
toDelete = xanListNew(
   allocFunction,
   freeFunction,
```

```
   NULL);
/* Compute the list of instructions to delete */
i = IRMETHOD_getFirstInstruction (
   method);
while (i != NULL){
   if (IRMETHOD_getInstructionType(i) == IRCALL){
      ir_method_t *calledMethod;
      JITUINT32 num;
      JITUINT32 resultType;

/* Fetch the called method */
calledMethod = IRMETHOD_getCalledMethod(
      method,
      i);

/* Ensure the called method is available *
   * in IR */
IRMETHOD_translateMethodToIR(
      calledMethod);

/* Fetch the type of the result of the *
   * called method */
resultType = IRMETHOD_getResultType(
      calledMethod);

/* Fetch the number of instructions of the *
   * called method */
num = IRMETHOD_getInstructionsNumber(
      calledMethod);

/* Fetch the first instruction of the *
   * called method */
firstInst = IRMETHOD_getFirstInstruction(
      method);
firstInstType = IRMETHOD_getInstructionType(
      firstInst);

/* Check if we can remove the call */
if ( (num == 1)&&
      (firstInstType == IRCALL) &&
      (resultType == IRVOID)){
   toDelete->append(toDelete, i);
}
}
```

```
  /* Fetch the next instruction */
  i = IRMETHOD_getNextInstruction (
    method,
    i);
}

/* Remove instructions */
item = toDelete->first(toDelete);
while (item != NULL){
  t_ir_instruction *inst;
  inst = item-> data;
  IRMETHOD_deleteInstruction(method, inst);
  item = item->next;
}

/* Free the memory */
toDelete->destroyList(toDelete);
}
```

The above code iterates over instructions that compose the method given as input; for each instruction, it checks whether it is a direct call to a method. Notice that in this case, it calls IRMETHOD_translateMethodToIR in order to ensure that the called method is available in IR language. This is necessary in case our code tool is used inside a dynamic compilation scheme, such as the JIT compilation, where there is no guarantee that called methods have been already translated to the IR language or not. In case the current call instruction points to a method that includes one single instruction, which is a return instruction (i.e., IRRET), this instruction is inserted inside a list, called toDelete, which is later used to optimize the code. After the set of instructions that we can safely remove from the code (i.e., the ones inside toDelete) are collected, our code tool removes them altogether.

Notice that our code tool builds a list of changes to apply to the code as a first step; only after this list of changes is known, it applies them altogether. This working scheme is common on code tools because in this way any information about the code requested by a given code tool is valid till that tool starts to change the code effectively; also, at that time, no information about the code is still needed, and therefore, no problem arises in case that information becomes invalid.

Chapter 7
Internal Structure

Abstract This book descrbied ILDJIT as a compilation framework, which can be used in order to either analyze or transform the code by providing extensions of it. This chapter describes internals of the framework that make possible its flexibility, which is a propriety exploited to make easier the implementation of these extensions.

Keywords Compiler internals · Compiler design choices

Previous chapters described how ILDJIT can be used to compile the input bytecode to machine code by using different compilation schemes and different code transformations provided by the framework. Also, how ILDJIT can be extended is described to customize the framework to best match the user needs. In this chapter, the internal structure of ILDJIT is described starting from an overview of the structure leading to a description of its main components.

7.1 Overview

The primary task of a compiler that targets bytecode languages is to translate each piece of the bytecode to a semantically equivalent target code to be directly executed by the hardware. Hereafter, we consider the CIL as input language because it is the bytecode fully supported by ILDJIT. Notice that by relying on ILDJIT technology, more bytecode languages can be supported (like the Java bytecode).

ILDJIT is designed with the key goals of flexibility, adaptability and modularity without compromising performance. Following, we discuss the two primary design decisions that shape the software architecture of ILDJIT: the choice of the basic translation unit and the modular architecture of the system.

S. Campanoni, *Guide to ILDJIT*, SpringerBriefs in Computer Science,
DOI: 10.1007/978-1-4471-2194-7_7, © Simone Campanoni 2011

7.1.1 Translation Unit

Choosing the correct granularity for the translation process is especially important in a dynamic compiler [1]. The function, or method, is generally taken as the natural unit [2]. A larger translation unit may provide additional optimization opportunities, but also imposes a higher risk of compiling code that will not be executed.

On the other hand, a smaller translation unit allows the compiler to output the translated code earlier, but heavily limits optimization, forcing the compiler to generate additional code to cope with frequent interruptions of execution. Specifically, if the unit is smaller than an entire function or method, then the computation state must be explicitly saved when switching between parts of a function that belong to different compilation units. In the other case this is not needed, since the function call boundary naturally defines a state to be preserved across a call (parameters and return values), while most of the local state can be destroyed (local variables of the callee).

In the case of CLI or Java, another, language-specific, reason candidates the CIL method for the role of translation unit. The metadata stored inside each CIL bytecode file assume the method as the main compilation unit, so that most information (local variables, stack size) is stored in a method-wise fashion.

ILDJIT uses a flexible translation unit. The method is taken as the *minimum* translation unit. The choice of larger units is possible at runtime, on a case by case basis: a policy can be set inside the optimization levels plugin, which can inline methods by calling the appropriate code tool (see Chap. 4). Moreover, in a component-based software, where a component must be deployed to a different processor, the union of methods of a given component can be considered as a single translation unit.

In the rest of the book, we will focus on individual methods, as they are the most common translation units.

Given this choice, there is a need to manage the invocation of not yet translated methods, when using lazy compilation [3], that is a method is only translated when one of its call points is first reached by the control flow. ILDJIT uses the traditional *trampoline* technique [3] to redirect such invocations to its own translation modules. After producing and installing the machine code translation of the invoked method, the call to the trampoline code is replaced with the actual memory address of the newly translated method.

Note that a trampoline has to be transparent to both caller and callee. While the caller is not supposed to perform any special check in passing parameters, the callee should not worry about the return value and the return address. The need for having different trampolines for different methods (as opposed to a single dispatch function in static compilation) comes from this principle.

7.1.2 Software Architecture

Here we provide an overview of the software architecture. ILDJIT is composed by the modules, or components, shown in Fig. 7.1.

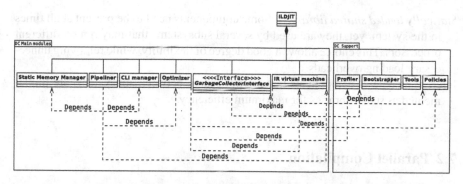

Fig. 7.1 UML class diagram of ILDJIT software architecture. Dependences to the Tools, Profiler and Garbage collector are not shown (all modules depend)

These modules can be divided into two groups: (1) the main components of the compiler system, including the Pipeliner, CLI manager, optimizer, garbage collector (GC) and IR virtual machine; and (2) the DC support infrastructure, including the profiling infrastructure (*Profiler*), the initialization subsystem (*Bootstrapper*), the data structure and support libraries (*Tools*) and finally the various policies (*Policies*). The latter ones will not be described in detail, being typical implementations of their class, with the exception of specific critical policies that affect the behavior of one of the main modules.

We provide a synthetic description of those modules whose name is not self-explanatory.

Pipeliner   implements and manages the software pipeline needed for the transla-
    tions, optimizations and executions of the CIL bytecode.
CLI manager   provides the functionalities needed to implement the CLI architecture
    and to translate the CIL bytecode to our IR language
IR virtual   machine translation of the IR code to the machine code and invocation of
    the latter.
Profiler   profiling functionalities for the internal modules of ILDJIT, as well as for
    the dynamically generated code .

Each module will be covered in its own section, to highlight the specificities of ILDJIT with respect to typical dynamic compilers.

Finally, each module is further modularized by using the following approaches, depending on its typical use:

Dynamically loaded shared library.   This choice gives the highest degree of flex-
    ibility, allowing the module to be loaded at runtime. It is therefore employed for
    all components that can be freely replaced, added or removed from the system.
    This choice allows the implementation of a plugin framework, making the DC
    customizable for a specific application domain (e.g. for multimedia components).

Statically loaded shared library.   Some components need to be present at all times
in the system, yet, they are used by several subsystems that may run on different
processors. This choice allows a good degree of flexibility, while removing unnecessary loading overheads.

Internal module   components that are not shared between subsystems are implemented as static libraries for maximum efficiency.

7.2 Parallel Compilation

In traditional Just-in-time compilers, the lazy compilation policy is adopted: when
the control flow leads to a method not yet compiled, the application is suspended,
and the method is translated. Given sufficient hardware resources, our DC can translate methods *before* the application invokes them, by parallelizing the application
execution and dynamic compilation tasks. In this case, application execution does
not yield to compilation. In the optimal case, the execution profile matches that of a
statically compiled program.

Translation, optimization and execution of CIL code are managed by an internal
software pipeline, designed not only to perform compilation and execution in parallel,
but also to exploit pipeline parallelism between different compilation and optimization phases.

The pipeline model exposes five stages as shown in Fig. 7.2. All stages can be
parallelized, if hardware resources are available. Each stage can be performed by
several parallel threads, possibly running on different CPUs, in order to simultaneously translate several CIL code pieces to IR. Similarly, several translation steps
from IR to machine code may run in parallel.

The Pipeliner module adaptively controls the amount of computing resources
allocated to the various dynamic compilation and optimization stages thus allowing
ILDJIT to quickly react to variations in the workload. In case of light machine load,
ILDJIT effectively hides the compilation overhead by ahead-of-time compilation of
methods that are expected to be invoked soon. When the load is heavier, it can reduce
resource usage by falling back to lazy compilation.

7.2.1 Dynamic Lookahead Compilation

A critical decision is which method to compile ahead of time. To tackle this issue, we
have developed a technique termed Dynamic Lookahead Compilation [4]. It employs
a combination of criteria that estimate the likelihood that a method m_i will be invoked
during the execution of method m_j, and estimate the distance between m_i and m_j
as the shortest weighted path over the call graph between the two methods.

ILDJIT monitors the executing CIL method and computes the distance to other
methods composing the application. All the CIL methods within a threshold D

Fig. 7.2 The translation pipeline model: on the *left*, the translation pipeline stages; on the *right*, the modules that implement the various stages; in the *rounded boxes* the state of the method code at the beginning of each stage

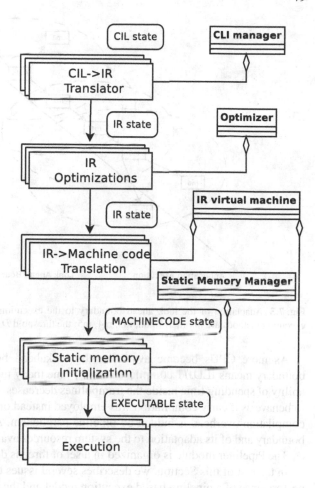

distance from the current method are candidates for translation and optimization. The rational of the distance based selection criterion is rather obvious: a method at near to zero distance will be probably required in the near future for execution, therefore it should be promptly translated to machine code to avoid a trampoline stall. Conversely, methods at greater distance do not need to be translated early, and the probability of them being requested in the future may be low. The threshold D is adjusted at runtime depending on available free CPUs'.

We define the *lookahead boundary* as the portion of the call graph of the application code, that includes the next candidate methods for compilation and optimization tasks. The lookahead boundary is a dynamic set, moving along with the executing method at a distance depending on the threshold D and available system resources (e.g., processing units dedicated to compilation tasks). An example of lookahead boundary and of its adaptation to the evolution of the execution of the application is shown in Fig. 7.3; in this example the system resources available are considered constant as the threshold D.

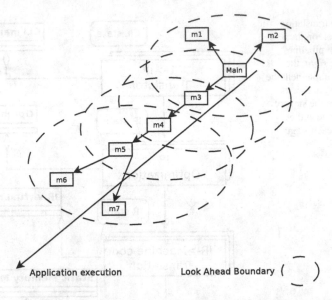

Fig. 7.3 Adaptation of the look ahead boundary to the execution of the application code; the executing methods are in order: Main, m3, m4, m5; the threshold D is 2, constant

As more CPUs become available, the lookahead boundary widens; a large boundary means ILDJIT compiles ahead of time many methods and then the probability of spending time inside the trampolines decreases—thus, the system appears to behave as if early compilation was employed instead of lazy compilation, but the compilation overhead is hidden by pipeline parallelism. An example of lookahead boundary and of its adaptation to the system resources available is shown in Fig. 7.4.

The Pipeliner module is organized in a set of threads depicted in Fig. 7.5.

In the rest of this Section, we describes several issues that affect correctness and performance of a pipeline-based execution model and the implementation strategies adopted in the Pipeliner modules to tackle them.

7.2.2 Compilation Load Balancing

Load balancing is essential to obtain good performance improvements while minimizing the overhead. In the Pipeliner module, thread pools are used to minimize the overhead of the threading subsystem over the compilation time, and an adaptive strategy is employed to manage the size of the thread pools.

Four thread pools corresponding to the first four stages of the pipeline shown in Fig. 7.2 contain, respectively: the CIL to IR translation threads; the IR optimizer threads; the IR to machine code translation threads; and the Static memory initialization threads. Each thread implements a single stage of the pipeline model working on a given translation unit.

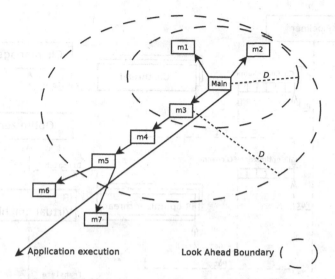

Fig. 7.4 Look ahead boundary with adaptive threshold D; D evolves from 2 to 3; the executing methods are in order: Main, m3

The number of threads in each thread pool is adaptively chosen, taking into account the hardware resources and the current compilation workload. The number of threads ranges, for all pools, between a maximum and minimum threshold, chosen at deployment time to exploit knowledge of the underlying platform.

The Pipeliner dynamically adapts the number of threads assigned to each stage of the pipe, using the hysteretic model shown in Fig. 7.6. The number of threads of stage i depends only on the number of methods in the pipe between stages i and $i - 1$. The choice of an hysteretic model rather than a linear one is due to the non-negligible cost of creating and deleting threads, which makes a conservative policy more appealing.

7.2.3 Static Memory Initialization

In object-oriented programming languages, it is possible to define fields for both instance and class. The latter are static fields that are allocated at class loading time. Their content is implicitly initialized before the first access, and the values are preserved across method calls and class instantiation. In CIL, a class can define a special method `cctor` used to perform the initialization of the class fields.

In the Pipeliner module, the static memory initialization step is the final stage of the compilation pipeline. At this stage, the `cctor` methods containing for each static memory area the initialization operations are invoked directly from the Pipeliner.

When a method enters the compilation pipeline, a list of required `cctor` methods is fetched and appended to its description. When the method reaches the last stage of

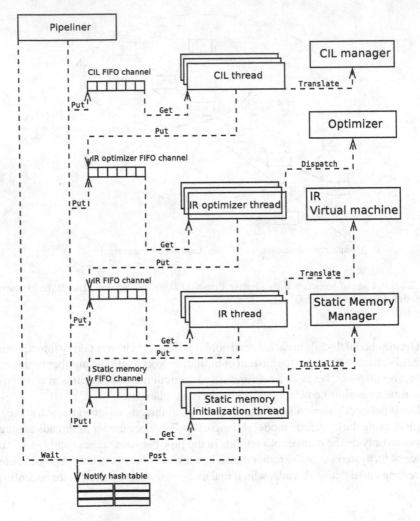

Fig. 7.5 The Pipeliner structure

the pipeline, all cctor methods are fetched, and, if they have not yet been executed, they are compiled and invoked.

However, this mechanism is vulnerable to deadlock when it interacts with compilation load balancing based on a thread pool.

Consider the case of a set of classes $S = \{C_1, \ldots, C_{|S|}\}$, where $|S|$ is greater than the number n_t of threads available in the last stage of the Pipeliner. Assume that for all classes $C_i \in \{C_1, \ldots, C_{|S|-1}\}$, C_i contains the initialization of one of its own class fields using the value of a class field of C_{i+1}. Then, if C_1 is the first class to be referenced by a method m of a class C_0 not in S, thread T_0 (assuming the whole Pipeliner system to be empty at the beginning of the operation) will hold m, waiting

Fig. 7.6 Pattern for threads adapting in the pipeline software

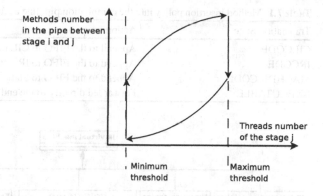

for the translation and invocation of the $\mathtt{cctor}$ method of C_1, then thread T_1 will be used to held that $\mathtt{cctor}$ method. Consequently, each thread T_i, $i \in [0, n_t)$ will be used to held $\mathtt{cctor}$ method of C_i, and the whole system will exhaust the set of available threads, but the $\mathtt{cctor}$ method of C_{n_t} will need the compilation of the $\mathtt{cctor}$ method of C_{n_t+1}, since $n_t < |S|$. In this case, the whole system goes into a deadlock.

To avoid this deadlock issue, we do not use the load balancing mechanism described in Sect. 7.2.2 in the last stage of the pipeline.

7.2.4 Threads Communication

The communication between consecutive stages of the pipeline is handled by asynchronous message passing, using software FIFO pipes allocated in shared memory between the threads of the Pipeliner module.

Even though items in each pipe are handled in a FIFO way, there is no guarantee that ordering of methods is preserved, since multiple threads are active at each stage, with potentially different execution times. However, out of order completion of the compilation process is not an issue except in specific cases, such as the static memory initialization, which are handled with ad hoc mechanisms, as shown in Sect. 7.2.3.

7.2.5 Pipeline Entry

The Pipeliner takes as input a CIL method to translate. Depending on the current *method translation state*, the Pipeliner selects the correct entry point: e.g., if a method has been already translated to IR, then the translated method can be directly moved to the optimization stage. Table 7.1 reports the action taken in each method translation state.

Table 7.1 Method insertion policy into the compilation pipeline as function of the translation state

Translation State	Action
CILCODE	Append to the FIFO to CIL translation threads
IRCODE	Append to the FIFO to IR optimizer threads
MACHINECODE	Append to the FIFO to Static memory initialization threads
EXECUTABLE	Forwarded directly to the end of the pipeline

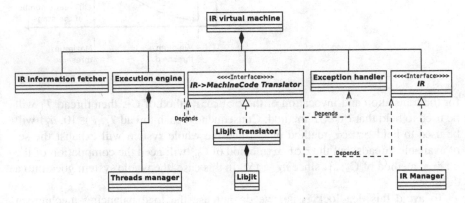

Fig. 7.7 UML class diagram of the IR virtual machine

The Pipeliner can be called synchronously or asynchronously. In the former case, it returns to the callee only when the input method is ready to be executed. In the latter case, the Pipeliner puts the method on the right FIFO, according to its translation state, and returns immediately to the callee.

Synchronous calls are performed by the Execution engine module of the IR virtual machine to translate methods that must be immediately executed.

Asynchronous calls are performed by the CIL $\rightarrow$ IR translator when a method call is found in the method under translation, and it is foreseen to be taken in the near future according to the distance estimation.

7.3 IR and Virtual Machine

Since most optimizations are done on the Intermediate Representation and the execution of the program is guaranteed by the *IR virtual machine* module, in this section we provide details.

The current implementation of the IR virtual machine exploits a very high degree of modularity and task parallelism. Its design has been thought in order to improve adaptability and flexibility. As shown in Fig. 7.7, the IR virtual machine is composed by six submodules which are further described in Sect. 7.3.1.

By applying the concept of separation of concerns, several steps of the translation process are delegated to submodules. In fact, the virtual machine implements the delegation pattern [5]: the single instance of IR virtual machine holds a reference to each submodule. During the translation process, the IR virtual machine orchestrates the interactions between its submodules by accessing to functionalities exposed via well defined interfaces. The life interval of each submodule may not exceed the life interval of the IR virtual machine.

As a result of the design, the IR virtual machine can be implemented in a highly parallel and modular way. When feasible, submodules may work in parallel cooperating with each other. The computation of each submodule is triggered by explicit requests coming from the IR virtual machine instance.

Submodules are also responsible of: management of exceptional behaviors in the executed code; initialization of static memory; fetching information about IR data types and methods.

At runtime, the Pipeliner module asks the virtual machine for the translation of IR methods interacting with the IR virtual machine interface. IR virtual machine internal modules are not visible from the outside.

7.3.1 IR Virtual Machine Components

The translation from IR to the machine code is handled through the *IR → Machine code translator* interface, relying on the code generator installed inside the system. Currently, ILDJIT provides the *Libjit Translator* module, which relies on Libjit [6], a code generator library.

In order to minimize the time spent for code generation, the IR language has been designed to be RISC like. Moreover, *IR → Machine code translator* may enable machine dependent optimizations according to the policy provided by the optimizations level plugin described in Chap. 4

The *Libjit Translator* module translates methods by simply interacting with Libjit through its API. Libjit provides currently supports x86, EM64T, ARM926 [7] and Alpha ISA.

The *Execution engine* module is in charge of executing the translated machine code. A method translated to machine code can be requested for execution by the IR virtual machine module. At runtime, the execution of a method can be paused to allow the translation of other methods through the use of trampolines as discussed in Sect. 7.1.1. A trampoline for a method that has never been compiled, implicitly triggers a translation request to the IR virtual machine. The main difference from a typical Just-In-Time compiler is that the translation and the execution phases are performed in parallel.

The Execution engine module includes the threading management capability which is provided by its *Threads manager* submodule. Currently the mapping between the IR and the OS threads used for them is bijective and it relies on the thread Posix library.

The *Exception handler* module supports the runtime exception handling mechanism. At runtime, a method may raise exception instances. Thus, the IR execution model gives the possibility to implement a unique handler routine for each method executed. When an exception is thrown at runtime, the execution is transferred to the handler of the function. The handler acts as a exceptions dispatcher: each exception instance is passed to a protected block of code either a catch, a filter or a finally block of code. If the function does not provide any protected region, the IR dispatcher ensures that the exception is propagated outside the method. The exception model is similar to the model specified in [8] albeit on our model there is only one exception handler for each method and there is not the possibility of bypassing the handler if an exception has been raised inside an exception block (what Lee called the *exc_signal* instruction). The implementation of the IR exception handling model is based on long jump machine code instructions.

Finally, the *IR Manager* module handles the modification of the IR methods (e.g. insert, remove, modify an instruction).

7.4 Extensible Framework

Code optimization is a critical feature for a DC. On one hand, more optimization opportunities arise at runtime, on the other hand, optimization is often costly. Thus, balancing the costs and benefits of optimization is of capital importance in a DC.

ILDJIT optimizes both at IR and target code level. The rationale for this choice is that higher-level transformation are easier to apply when the semantic information of the source program is still available. For instance, array references are clearly recognizable, instead of being a sequence of low-level address calculations [9]. Machine-dependent optimization are, of course, performed at the target code level. An example of transformation that is useful at both levels is loop-invariant code motion, which can be applied both at IR level to expressions and at machine code level to address computations. The latter is particularly relevant when indexing multidimensional arrays [9].

In both cases, the transformation does not change the code level, so optimizing an IR method yields another IR method, and optimizing a target machine method yields another target machine method.

To allow the exploration of the cost-benefit trade-off, ILDJIT implements a modular and extensible framework where each optimization pass is structured as a plugin called code tool already described in Chap. 6.

The use of plugins forces ILDJIT to rely on indirect call mechanisms to transfer information between optimization passes and intermediate representation. While this choice may seem suboptimal, we found experimental evidence [10] that show that the performance degradation is not significant.

Finally, to maximize the benefits reaped from the availability of runtime information, ILDJIT implements adaptive optimization by means of optimization levels plugins described in Chap. 4.

The rest of this section describes the optimization framework.

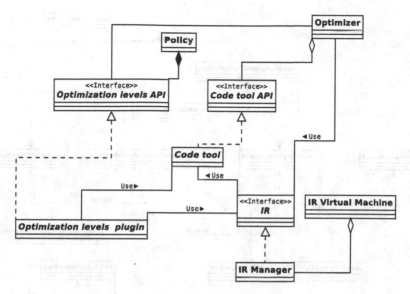

Fig. 7.8 UML class diagram of the optimization interfaces and modules

7.4.1 Interfaces

To obtain good modularity, ILDJIT defines four interfaces, shown in Fig. 7.8.

An internal module, *Optimizer*, is the bridge between code tools and the rest of ILDJIT.

The *IR API* provides the optimization plugins with the ability to manipulate IR methods by adding, deleting, modifying or moving IR instructions.

The *Optimization Levels API* defines the contract between ILDJIT and the optimization levels plugins.

Finally, the *code tool API* is a goal-oriented, bidirectional interface that allows plugins to state their own requirements without declaring how to achieve them. This information is necessary to allow optimization plugins to rely on the results of analysis (or other optimization) plugins. E.g., a forward propagation plugin may require data-flow information, without knowing which data-flow analysis plugin will compute it.

To this end, the code tool API defines a set of high-level pre-defined optimization tasks (e.g. instruction scheduling) which are used by the external plugins to declare their targets as well as their dependencies. Through the code tool API, ILDJIT can introspect optimization plugins, and, conversely, each plugin can request information from the DC. For instance, code tools can request ILDJIT to invoke another plugin that satisfies a given dependency, such as computing available expressions, without knowing beforehand which plugin has the appropriate capabilities.

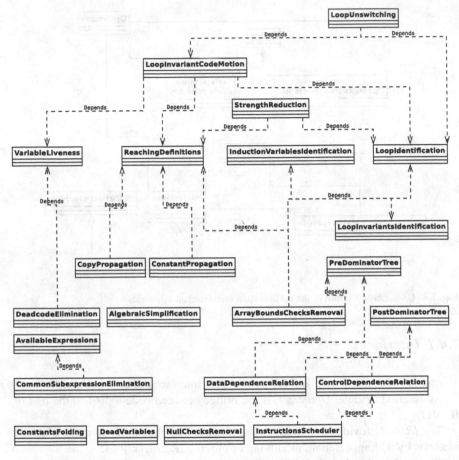

Fig. 7.9 UML class diagram of the optimization plugins and their dependences

ILDJIT uses the information obtained through the code tool API to construct a dependency graph among the optimization plugins, and it verifies that all dependencies can actually be satisfied.

Figure 7.9 shows the dependency graph for the currently available code tools.

7.5 Input Language

The CLI manager module (Fig. 7.10) is in charge of managing the CIL bytecode according the ECMA-335 specification, to:

- Load and decode CIL files;
- Translate CIL methods in an intermediate representation (our IR language);
- Recognize, decode and create instances of built-in and user defined value types;

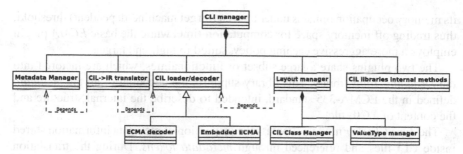

Fig. 7.10 UML class diagram of the CLI manager software architecture

- Inspect metadata tables in order to retrieve memory layout informations for both CIL classes and value-types;
- Support the CLI exception handling model;
- Provide the implementations of various internal calls of the C# base class library.

Note that ECMA-335 identifies two subsets of the common language infrastructure (CLI): the *managed* and the *unmanaged* code. Our experience is that implementing the support for both of them makes the project complexity much larger than the sum of the two isolated cases. In our experience, managed and unmanaged support require 2 and 1 person-years respectively, when developed independently, but their integration brings the total development time to 7 person-years. More precisely, the following issues should be taken into consideration:

- ECMA-335 allows objects to be moved from the managed to the unmanaged code—in this case, the GC must not consider that object anymore;
- To support aggressive optimization as well as precise garbage collection, the DC must take into account whether a pointer points to an object, a field, or an unmanaged data item, which increases the complexity of the internal type set.
- The DC has to provide facilities to support transition of the execution between the two subsets, including marshaling and unmarshaling of the parameters and platform dependent invocation.

7.5.1 Load and Decode Tasks

Loading and decoding of CIL files is performed by external modules (*plugins*) that implement an interface. In addition to the modularity benefits inherent in the use of interfaces, plugins provide adaptability and extensibility to support, e.g., non-standard extensions to the CIL bytecode produced by specific front-end compilers.

Currently, ILDJIT includes two loading and decoding plugins, *ECMA* and *Embedded ECMA*. The two differ in the data caching policies: the *Embedded ECMA* decoding plugin implements a more restrictive policy, only caching information while its memory occupation remains under a given (target machine-dependent) threshold, thus trading off memory space for computation time, while the basic *ECMA* plugin employs a more aggressive caching policy, suited to high-end targets.

The two plugins share a large subset of functionalities, which are factored into the *Decoding Tools* library. This library supports the decoding of all the *metadata* defined in the ECMA-335 standard, intended to describe the internal structure and the content of a CIL file.

The *Type Checker* module supports the inspection of metadata information stored inside CLI files and referenced through *metadata tokens*. During the translation phase, the CLI manager frequently needs to retrieve metadata information for value and reference types, which represent semantic information behind the type identifier (e.g., which interfaces a class type implements, or whether a type is an interface or a class).

Basically, *Type Checker* provides functions that can be used to check whether a property is held by a given type.

Type Checker has been implemented in a highly modular way, hiding the implementation logic behind the easy-to-use interfaces. The behavior of each function exposed by the interface can be redefined in order to allow adaptability and flexibility. For example, it is possible to implement metadata caching policies for systems where memory space is critical, and not all tables can be kept in memory at the same time.

Thus, multiple *Type Checker* module instances can be provided, with a runtime selection of the instance actually used. At the present time, this decision is performed implicitly when the *ECMA* plugin or the *Embedded ECMA* plugin are loaded into the system.

Moreover, Type Checker can be extended to support future CLI formats containing custom metadata tables, and is the only part of the compiler that needs to be modified to this end.

7.5.2 Layout Manager

ECMA-335 [4] standardizes the layout of data structures in a memory managed heap. To create valid instances of a given class or value type in memory, the DC needs information from the `ClassLayout` metadata table, accessed through the Type Checker.

The `ClassLayout` table holds an entry for each type that requires special constraints on how fields of valid instances should be laid out in memory. If this entry is not present for a type, then the loader module is free to decide how to layout in memory instances of that class.

To accomplish its main goal, the Layout Manager interacts directly with the loading and decoding plugin as well as the Type Checker module, and computes the relative offset of each field with respect to the header of the instance in memory. It also defines a *virtual table* containing all the references to method functions implemented by a class or value type.

Layout Manager behaves as an interface between the *IR Virtual Machine* and the memory layout information. The Layout Manager decouples functional issues (the correctness of the translation process performed by IR virtual machine) from performance issues, i.e., the trade-off between computing on-demand and caching layout information for rarely used classes and types. The on-demand computation of rarely used information is especially important for memory size optimization in the compilation of CLI programs, which can access very large libraries such as the mscorlib core library—caching layout information for all types defined in such libraries would lead to huge memory occupation. The Layout Manager therefore implements different caching policies tailored to the usage patterns of classes and types.

The interaction of Layout Manager and Garbage Collection is limited to the communication of the object size to the Layout Manager. Thus, the GC interface and implementation are much simpler, since all layout issues are handled in a separate module.

To guarantee maximum performance, when there are no constraints on layout imposed by CLI to preserve low-level source language semantics, it is possible to dynamically redefine the layout policy. This requires that cached information for live objects be preserved across the redefinition, but allows to progressively change the policy as old objects are deallocated. Layout Manager thus implements the *strategy* design pattern [5].

When the IR virtual machine needs to create instances of value types on the stack, it interacts with a subcomponent of the Layout Manager, called *ValueType Manager*. The IR language implemented by the IR virtual machine knows how to allocate *Built-in Value Types* on the stack, since their size is known, but does not have the same kind of information about *User Defined Value Types*. Thus, the IR virtual machine exposes an interface to explicitly manage the allocation of data elements onto the execution stack, and calls the ValueType Manager to perform this task.

7.5.3 Exception Manager

This module supports the creation of CLI exception instances and implements the exception handling mechanism. The current implementation is based on long jump mechanism.

The Exception Manager gets from the Type Checker the metadata for predefined exceptions (*CLI exceptions*) as well as the handler information, and packages them to speed up the generation of exception instances. Exception instances encapsulate information on the *exceptional behaviors* that affect the control flow, including a call stack image describing the site where the exceptional behavior was generated.

The module services are used by the IR virtual machine to raise exceptions and to trigger the execution of the exception handling procedure.

Finally, the exception handling mechanism directs the routing of the exception instances at runtime to the handlers. This operation is non-trivial, since

ECMA-335 allows multiple handlers per method, while the IR virtual machine supports the definition of at most one exception handler per IR method. To bridge this gap, the IR exception handler must explicitly implement the control logic needed to dispatch an exception instance to the correct piece of IR code that implements the handler.

System.OutOfMemoryException instances are used to notify that there is not enough memory at runtime to fulfill a request of allocation for a new object into a managed memory heap. In this case, a System.OutOfMemoryException instance is created and implicitly thrown by the IR virtual machine.

In our opinion, even though the System.OutOfMemoryException is classified as an exception in the ECMA-335 specification, it is more a runtime error than a typical exception. Moreover, its peculiarities make it difficult to manage it properly. Indeed, the creation of an instance of this exception requires a memory allocation, which may result in another out of memory exception, leading to an endless loop. This issue is well known in Java virtual machine implementations as well. In some JVM implementations [11], GC fail to return a valid reference when the exception instance is created, leading to catastrophic errors.

A possible solution consists of handling a System.OutOfMemoryException as an error, avoiding the endless loop issue, but would not result in a compliant implementation of the ECMA-335 exception handling model, where all exceptions are catchable.

Currently, IR virtual machine provides the following behavior. A request of memory allocation for a new instance in memory is always forwarded to the GC. If the memory allocation fails, the runtime system triggers the creation of a System.OutOfMemoryException instance. This assumes there is enough free memory to create a System.OutOfMemory Exception. If this is not the case, the IR virtual machine does not raise a second exception instance, returning instead a singleton instance of System.OutOfMemoryException pre-allocated at bootstrap time.

As long as System.OutOfMemoryException can still be catched there is a strong possibility that other by memory exceptions be thrown out from the handler code. In this case, not providing a distinct System.OutOfMemoryException instance for each exception raised means there is no way to produce always a valid stack trace—which is required by the specification.

However, having pre-allocated an instance of System.OutOfMemory Exception at bootstrap time, the IR Virtual Machine prevents the endless creation of out of memory exceptions, while introducing only a minor discrepancy from ECMA-335.

7.5.4 Internal Methods

In ECMA-335, a CIL method is said to be *internal* if only its signature is present in CIL language, while the body has to be supplied by the DC. A static compiler,

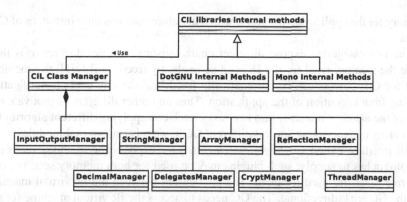

Fig. 7.11 UML class diagram of the CLI internal methods module

when it generates the CIL assembly for a given source program (e.g. a C# program), must mark internal methods with the appropriate tag. Tags are needed by the DC for linking purposes.

Any static compiler must choose an implementation of the Base Class Library (BCL) (which is a set of CIL classes described in the ECMA standard) and therefore implicitly chooses the set of internal methods to be supplied by the DC.

As a consequence, the CIL programs are to some extent *Compiler-dependent*, or more precisely, *BCL-dependent*. Moreover, since the bodies of the internal methods have to be supplied by every DC, then they are replicated on them.

ILDJIT addresses this problem by providing the *CIL libraries Internal Methods* module, whose class diagram is shown in Fig. 7.11. Our solution is based on the *CIL Class Manager* module, which supplies the functionalities needed to implement the DC-dependent actions, like allocation of a new object or determination of the offset of a given field of a CIL class. In this way, each BCL can be supported by ILDJIT providing a new sub-class of *CIL libraries Internal Methods*.

All sub-classes of *CIL libraries Internal Methods* are BCL-independent and provide the bodies of the internal methods. Whenever they need to do some DC-dependent action, they rely on the class *CIL Class Manager*.

Currently, ILDJIT provides two Internal Method classes: *Mono Internal Methods* and *DotGNU Internal Methods*. The names show which BCL they target.

7.6 Memory Management

The GC module provides a range of memory management functionalities. The simplest service is to allocate memory portions to programs at their request, and to free them for reuse when no longer needed. ECMA-335 allows a memory portion to be declared no longer useful automatically or explicitly. Memory requests may be classified as: first, memory for the internal modules of the dynamic compiler; second, memory for the application program, which therefore contains only instances of CIL classes.

The two categories expose different characteristics. A chief difference is that, while the memory used for the DC can be explicitly freed by ILDJIT, the memory used for CIL objects can be automatically freed, without any explicit notification coming from execution of the application. Thus and other differences motivate our split of the memory manager into two tasks, each one applying different algorithms.

In order to experiment several different GC's, we rely on external modules.

An interface called *GarbageCollectorInterface* exposes the methods that each GC plugin has to supply; such plugins may be used for both memory sets, but two separate heaps are used for them. The interactions between the IR virtual machine and the GC are bidirectional. The GC needs to access the IR virtual machine for the following reasons:

- to request the computation of the root set [12];
- to find the objects referenced by the current one;
- to check if an object can be moved from a memory location to another one (some objects may be constrained [4]);
- to call finalizer methods for the objects marked as garbage by the GC itself.

The above tasks are demanded to the VM because the GC does not known:

- the stack frame of the methods in order to compute the root set;
- the layout of the objects to compute the list of objects reachable at one step by a generic object;
- how-to translate and execute a CIL method.

These tasks can be performed by the IR virtual machine.

All memory allocations are recorded by the GC to speed up the collection and make it precise [12]. Each garbage collection plugin manages the memory using a heap with a fixed size set by the bootstrapper module. The root set is managed using a dynamic array of pointers.

Since memory management greatly affects performances, and the effectiveness of different garbage collection algorithms varies depending on the memory access patterns, ILDJIT includes several garbage collection plugins. Currently, the user can choose among the following plugins, as shown in Fig. 7.12:

MarkAndSweep implements the mark and sweep algorithm [12];
MarkCompact implements the mark compact GC algorithm [12];
Copy implements the copying GC algorithm [12];
Bdw is a wrapper for the GC of Boehm, Demers and Weiser [13], which is based on the mark and sweep algorithm, but supports extensions for generational GC.

The memory management system can be configured by the user to employ a different GC for application data than Bdw, which is always used for internal data. When used for internal data, Bdw is configured to perform non-generational collection, since the allocation and deallocation patterns of the ILDJIT internal data are simple enough that the more complex policy would not give any benefit. For the

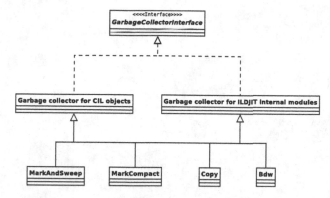

Fig. 7.12 UML class diagram of the garbage collector module

instances of CIL classes, on the other hand, the default configuration uses Mark-Compact. MarkCompact has the advantage of improving locality with respect to MarkAndSweep or Bdw, without increasing the memory requirements as the Copy collector does.

References

1. Duesterwald, E.: Dynamic compilation, pp. 739–761. CRC Press (2003)
2. Toshio, S., Toshiaki, Y., Nakatani Toshio N.: A region-based compilation technique for dynamic compilers. ACM Trans. Progr. Lang. Syst. (28): 134–174 (2006)
3. Krintz, C., Grove, D., Lieber, D., Sarkar, V., Calder, B.: Reducing the overhead of dynamic compilation. Softw. Pract. Experience. (31): 717–738 CRC press, (2001)
4. Campanoni, S., Sykora, M., Agosta, G., Crespi-Reghizzi, S.: Dynamic look ahead compilation: a technique to hide jit compilation latencies in multicore environment. International Conference on Compiler Construction. pp. 220–235 (2009)
5. Gamma, E., Helm, R., Johnson, R., Vlissides, J.: Design patterns: elements of reusable object-oriented software. Addison-Wesley, Reading (1995)
6. Southern Storm Software. DotGNU project. http://www.dotgnu.org Accessed 11 June 2011 (2008)
7. Tartara, M., Campanoni, S., Agosta, G., Crespi Reghizzi, S.: Just-in-time compilation on ARM processors. ICOOOLPS. pp. 70–73 (2009)
8. Lee, P.A.: Exception handling in C programs. Softw. Pract. Experience. (13): 389–405 (1983)
9. Bacon, D.F., Graham, S.L., Sharp, O.J.: Compiler transformations for high-performance computing. ACM Comput. Surveys. (26): 345–420 (1994)
10. Campanoni, S., Agosta, G., Crespi-Reghizzi, S., Di Biagio, A.: A highly flexible, parallel virtual machine: design and experience of ILDJIT. Softw. Pract. Experience. (40): 177–207 (2010)
11. Agosta, G., Crespi Reghizzi, S., Svelto, G.: Jelatine: a virtual machine for small embedded systems. JTRES. (40): 170–177 (2006)
12. Wilson, P.R.: Uniprocessor garbage collection techniques. Workshop on Memory Management (1992)
13. Boehm, H.J., Weiser, M.: Garbage collection in an uncooperative environment. Softw. Pract. Experience. (18): 807–820 (1988)

Appendix

Getting Help

If you encounter a problem not covered by this guide, there are technical materials you can read, which are listed on the ILDJIT website.

Alternatively, authors can be directly contacted through the standard mailing list of the project, which is available from the project website.

S. Campanoni, *Guide to ILDJIT*, SpringerBriefs in Computer Science,
DOI: 10.1007/978-1-4471-2194-7, © Simone Campanoni 2011